TOMORROW'S LAWYERS

Praise for *Tomorrow's Lawyers*:

'For years, Susskind has challenged lawyers to reinvent the way we work. Now, in *Tomorrow's Lawyers*, he presents his clearest picture yet of what the future has in store.'

Hugh Verrier, Chairman, White & Case

'A must-read for anyone interested in the future of legal services. Insightful, thought provoking and challenging, Susskind has clearly identified the inexorable forces that will drive change.'

David Allgood, Executive Vice President and
General Counsel, Royal Bank of Canada

'An invaluable resource for all participants in 21st century law. Susskind provides a uniquely expert, yet readable and succinct, analysis of the profound changes underway in the profession and business of law, including specific predictions of where it all is headed and concrete strategies for achieving rewarding outcomes.'

Ralph Baxter, Chairman and CEO, Orrick

'One of the legal world's most respected commentators, Richard Susskind, has amassed further compelling evidence of the need for a legal profession that extends itself beyond traditional service. *Tomorrow's Lawyers* is a must-read not only for those embarking on a legal career - but also acts as a timely reminder to practitioners who wish to stay ahead of the curve.'

Robert Gogel, CEO, Integreon

'In *Tomorrow's Lawyers*, Richard Susskind has managed to articulate the tremendous change facing the legal profession in a uniquely insightful way. He captures the challenges and opportunities for the lawyer of the future in the most readable form I have come across. This book is required reading for anyone interested in the business of law.'

Neville Eisenberg, Managing Partner,
Berwin Leighton Paisner LLP

TOMORROW'S LAWYERS
An Introduction to Your Future

Richard Susskind

OXFORD
UNIVERSITY PRESS

Great Clarendon Street, Oxford, OX2 6DP,
United Kingdom

Oxford University Press is a department of the University of Oxford.
It furthers the University's objective of excellence in research, scholarship,
and education by publishing worldwide. Oxford is a registered trade mark of
Oxford University Press in the UK and in certain other countries

First published 2013

Impression: 6

British Library Cataloguing in Publication Data

Data available

ISBN 978-0-19-966806-9

Printed in Great Britain by
Clays Ltd, St Ives plc

*I dedicate this book to
Daniel, Jamie, and Ali,
my loving children,
who bring me endless happiness*

PREFACE

I have written this book to provide tomorrow's lawyers and legal educators with an accessible account of the pressing issues that currently face the legal profession and the justice system. We are, I have no doubt, on the brink of fundamental change in the world of law, and my main aim is to encourage wider discussion of the forces at play and their likely impact.

Although originally conceived as a guide to the future for the next generation of lawyers, I expect that the book will also be read by more experienced practitioners. For busy professionals who do not have the time to read lengthy texts, I hope that it serves as a punchier version of my ideas than my previous work. Certainly, it represents a substantially updated version of my views on trends in the legal market.

I do not anticipate that readers will agree with all of what I say. But if the book gives rise to more serious reflection and debate about the future of the law and lawyers, then I have done my job. And yet, because we live in such rapidly shifting times, it is a job that is necessarily incomplete. Each day, I hear fresh tales of innovation in law—a new legal business here, an online facility there, and a regular flow of imaginative ideas for meeting clients' needs in different ways. In citing these innovations, I had to draw the line somewhere, however, and so I have only been able to refer to developments that surfaced before the end of May 2012. I would not be surprised, by the time this book is published, if some important new legal services have been launched in the interim.

I have some people to thank. First of all, there is the team at Oxford University Press. This is the fifth time that OUP has agreed to take on one of my books and, as ever, it has been a privilege to work with such a well-regarded publishing house. I am especially grateful to Ruth Anderson and Sophie Barham in the UK and to Ninell Silberberg in the US for their friendly support and advice. I must also record my thanks to the various referees who anonymously assessed my book proposal and made a wide range of suggestions that led, I believe, to many significant improvements.

Next is Patricia Cato, who helped me with innumerable initial drafts and still comfortably outperforms any speech recognition system in making sense of my rapid Glaswegian.

I have also benefited greatly from the guidance, encouragement, and criticisms of a small group of friends and colleagues who generously spent many hours of their time reading an early draft of the book—Neville Eisenberg, Hazel Genn, Daniel Harris, Laurence Mills, David Morley, Alan Paterson, and Tony Williams. To each, I extend my profound thanks.

Two reviewers deserve separate mention—my sons, Daniel and Jamie. This book would not have been written without their love and encouragement. They enthused when I came up with the idea of a book for aspiring lawyers, they motivated me when other commitments made it difficult to maintain momentum, and they commented extensively on earlier drafts. Their range and clarity of thought amaze me.

The last person but one to thank is Ali, my daughter and friend, to whom, along with her brothers, this book is dedicated. I cherish every one of the many companionable moments we spend together. I could not have a more wonderful daughter.

And finally, as always, I am very grateful to my loving wife, Michelle. For over 30 years now, she has indulgently endured my bouts of obsessive writing. It cannot be easy. Her boundless support for my work and her confidence in my ideas mean so very much to me.

Richard Susskind
June 2012
Radlett, England

When one door closes, another door opens; but we often look so long and so regretfully upon the closed door that we do not see the ones which open for us.

ALEXANDER GRAHAM BELL

Institutions will try to preserve the problem to which they are the solution.

CLAY SHIRKY

CONTENTS

INTRODUCTION

This book is a short introduction to the future for young and aspiring lawyers.

Tomorrow's legal world, as predicted and described here, bears little resemblance to that of the past. Legal institutions and lawyers are at a crossroads, I claim, and are poised to change more radically over the next two decades than they have over the last two centuries. If you are a young lawyer, this revolution will happen on your watch.

'Young' should be construed broadly, applying to students who are contemplating a job in law through to newly promoted partners in firms who are wondering how their careers might unfold. I also write for those who are interested in young legal businesses, such as the high-tech start-ups and the new-look law firms that are already seeking to redefine the legal marketplace.

To elder statesmen in traditional firms, who may feel after a couple of paragraphs that they are excused from reading on, I issue a warning. Although it may appear that the future, and particularly the topic of IT, is of interest primarily to the next generation, some of the transformations that I discuss here are coming in the next few years. Unless retirement is imminent, what I say here will directly affect older lawyers too. More than this, leaders in the legal profession today should be concerned not just about hanging on until their pensions click in, but about their long-term legacy as well.

'My call is to the young in heart, regardless of age,' John F. Kennedy once said, and I say this again now. I write primarily for the youthful of spirit, for the energetic, for the optimistic—for those who join me in recognizing that we can and should modernize our legal and justice systems.

Discontinuity in the Legal Profession

This book comes at a time of great debate in the legal world over an array of vital issues. There is deep concern, for example, about cuts in public legal funding that may reduce 'access to justice'. There are worries about law schools that seem to be offering places to students in greater numbers than there are job opportunities. And there is unease about the disproportionate cost of pursuing claims in the courts.

I offer remedies for these and many other ills, but I do not provide the same kinds of answer as those offered by most careers advisers, parents, professors, and legal practitioners. To give a flavour: while most lawyers are arguing for smaller cuts in legal aid, I argue we should be exploring and implementing alternative ways of providing legal guidance, not least through online legal services; while commentators agitate about over-recruitment into law schools, I identify a whole set of exciting new occupations for tomorrow's lawyers, although I am troubled that we are not preparing students and young practitioners for these jobs; and while judges and litigators are seeking to control the costs of litigation, I believe we should be introducing virtual hearings and online dispute resolution.

Most inhabitants of today's legal world tend to look for solutions by extrapolating from the past and on the assumption of continuity in the legal profession. In contrast, I foresee discontinuity over time and the emergence of a legal industry that will be quite alien to the current legal establishment. The future of legal service is neither Grisham nor Rumpole. Nor is it wigs, wood-panelled courtrooms, leather-bound tomes, or arcane legal jargon. It will not even be the now dominant model of lawyering, which is face-to-face, consultative professional service by advisers who meet clients in their offices, whether glitzy or dusty, and dispense tailored counsel. To meet the needs of clients, we will need instead to dispense with much of our current cottage industry and re-invent the way in which legal services are delivered. Just as other professions are undergoing massive upheaval, then the same must now happen in law. Indeed, it is already happening. The bespoke specialist who handcrafts solutions for clients will be challenged by new working methods, characterized by lower labour costs, mass customization, recyclable legal knowledge, pervasive use of IT, and more.

When I was at law school, in the late 1970s and early 1980s, few students gave much thought to what the future might hold for the legal profession. We took it for granted that the work of lawyers in, say, 25 years' time, would be much as it was in our time. It transpired that we were right to expect little change. In contrast, in looking 25 years ahead from now, I argue it would be absurd to expect lawyers and courts to carry on operating as they do now. If only because of the inexorable rise in the power and uptake of IT—to pick one of several drivers of change—we must surely expect something manifestly more than modest adjustment.

So Why Listen to Me?

You might think that hordes of senior people in the legal profession are currently thinking deeply about the long-term prospects for lawyers and the legal system. But almost no one you might expect to be at the helm—politicians, senior partners in law firms, policymakers, law professors, top judges, leaders of professional bodies—is looking much beyond the next few years. In these difficult economic times, the here-and-now seems to be providing headache enough.

In truth, in the legal community there are only a few dozen lawyers and professors around the world who are devoting their working lives to theorizing about and planning for the long term (most of their works are referenced in the Further Reading section of this book). I am one of them and have been writing, speaking, and advising on the future for longer than most. I started my journey in 1981, as a third-year undergraduate law student at the University of Glasgow. Since then, I have written a doctorate in law and computers at Oxford University, and worked for several years with one of the 'Big 4' accounting firms, and then for much of the 1990s with an international law firm, on whose board I sat for three years. I have been a law professor for over 20 years, and, for 15 years, an independent adviser to law firms, in-house legal departments, governments, and judiciaries around the world.

Even my fiercest critics will concede that in my numerous books and newspaper columns over the last 25 years I have been right more often than wrong in my predictions. So, I say this: if there is a better than even chance that the radically transformed legal world I predict will come to be, then it should be worth spending a few hours contemplating its implications. If my winning run continues—and my confidence in my predictions is greater now than in the 1990s—then it might pay dividends to read on. And my hope is that readers will not respond defensively ('how can we stop this happening?') but will find exciting new options and opportunities in these pages ('I want to be one of the pioneers').

How the Book is Organized

The book is divided into three main parts. The first is an updated, simplified restatement of my views on the future of legal services, as presented in three previous works—*The Future of Law* (1996), *Transforming the Law* (2000), and, especially, *The End of Lawyers?* (2008). I have tried to pick out and highlight, for young and aspiring lawyers, the key themes of these books. I introduce the main drivers of change in the legal market and explain why and how these will lead lawyers to work differently and will encourage new providers to enter the market with novel approaches to legal service. I also outline a large range of technologies that I believe will disrupt the traditional working practices of lawyers. My focus here, as throughout, is largely, but not exclusively, on civil work in commercial law firms. For readers who are already familiar with my ideas from my 2008 work, I urge you not to skip Part One, because there have been significant developments in the market and in my thinking since I wrote *The End of Lawyers?*

Next, in Part Two, I sketch out the new legal landscape, as I expect it to be. I discuss the future for law firms, the challenges facing in-house lawyers, and the likely progression of the shifts

I anticipate. I also lay out some of the ways in which 'access to justice' problems will be overcome through a variety of online legal services. And I offer some predictions too about the work of judges and the courts, and the promise of virtual hearings and online dispute resolution.

Finally, in the third part of the book, I focus more specifically on the prospects for young lawyers. I ask what new jobs and employers there will be and for what and how the next generation of lawyers will be trained. I provide optimistic and encouraging answers to these questions. I also equip young lawyers with some penetrating questions to put to their current and prospective employers. And I conclude by looking to the long term and putting down a challenge for young (in heart) lawyers everywhere.

Wayne Gretzky, perhaps the finest ice hockey player of all time, famously advised to 'skate where the puck's going, not where it's been'. Similarly, when lawyers are thinking about the future, whether about their law firms or law schools, they should be planning for the legal market as it will be and not as it once was. In ice hockey terms, however, most lawyers are currently skating to where the puck used to be. My purpose, then, is to show where that puck is most likely to end up.

PART ONE

Radical Changes in the Legal Market

1 | Three Drivers of Change

The legal market is in an unprecedented state of flux. Over the next two decades, the way in which lawyers work will change radically. Entirely new ways of delivering legal services will emerge, new providers will enter the market, and the workings of our courts will be transformed. Unless they adapt, many traditional legal businesses will fail. On the other hand, a whole set of fresh opportunities will present themselves to entrepreneurial and creative young lawyers.

I believe there will be three main drivers of change: the 'more-for-less' challenge, liberalization, and information technology. Other commentators may point to different factors, such as shifting demography and increasing globalization. I do not deny that such factors are significant but my specific focus here is on the changes that we will see in the way in which legal services are delivered; and all my research and advisory work, as well as what I have seen in other professions, lead me to the conviction that my three drivers are the ones to watch for. Let me introduce each in turn.

The 'More-for-Less' Challenge

Clients of lawyers come in many different forms. There are in-house lawyers, who work within large organizations and who spend mightily on legal advice when they have major disputes to resolve or large deals to conclude. There are managers within small or medium-sized businesses, who have properties to rent, employees to engage, and all manner of regulations with which to comply. And there are individual citizens, who may need legal help with such matters as moving house, coping with debt, or pursuing some personal injury claim. Although diverse in nature, these clients currently share a big challenge—generally, they cannot afford legal services when delivered in the traditional way.

General Counsel, the individuals who run in-house legal departments, invariably say that they face three problems. First of all, because of today's difficult economic conditions, they are under pressure to reduce the number of lawyers in their teams. Second, they are being asked by their chief executives, chief finance officers, and boards to reduce the amount they spend on external law firms. And yet, at the same time, third, they say they have more legal and compliance work to undertake than ever before; and that the work is riskier too. Many General Counsel confess that they are being required to reduce their overall legal budgets by between 30 per cent and 50 per cent. On the face of it, this is unsustainable. These clients from major companies and financial institutions are facing the prospect of an increasing workload and yet diminishing legal resources. Something surely has to give here. I call this problem the 'more-for-less' challenge—how can clients, working with their external law firms, deliver more legal services at less cost?

The more-for-less challenge is not just a conundrum for in-house lawyers. Small businesses face a similar dilemma. These traders do not have their own specialist in-house lawyers, and whenever they are in need of serious legal help, they must currently turn to external law firms. In these demanding times, however, many business people confess that they cannot afford lawyers and often have to run the risk of working without legal guidance. As for the consumer, although the law is central to all of our lives, dramatic decreases in public legal aid mean, effectively, that only the very rich or the very poor any longer have the means to afford the services of lawyers. Citizens face the more-for-less challenge too.

I believe the more-for-less challenge, above all others, will underpin and define the next decade of legal service. The more-for-less challenge will, I expect, irreversibly change the way that lawyers work.

Liberalization

The second main driver of change is liberalization. A little background should help here. In most countries, historically and generally speaking, only qualified lawyers have been permitted to provide legal services to clients, and, even then, only from specific types of organization (typically from partnerships). Laws and regulations have stipulated who can be a lawyer, who can run and own a legal business, and what services they can provide. Different countries have drawn lines in different places, so that, in England and Wales, what is known as 'reserved' legal business (work that only qualified lawyers are permitted to undertake) is a narrower category than the 'authorized practice of law', as it is known in the US. But the principles underlying the exclusivity of lawyers are similar in most jurisdictions; and the pivotal justification is that it is in clients' interests that those who advise them on the law are suitably trained and experienced. Just as we would not want any Joe performing brain surgery on us, then, similarly, we should not wish that same Joe representing us in the courtroom.

But one big problem here is that this closed community of legal specialists does not seem to offer sufficient choice to the consumer. For decades, this has led critics and reformers to claim that the legal profession is an unjustifiable monopoly and that its practices are restrictive and anti-competitive. In turn, many have campaigned for a relaxation of the laws and regulations that govern who can offer legal services and from what types of business. This is a call for liberalization. (Note that liberalization is not the same beast as de-regulation. Most campaigners for liberalization still want lawyers to be regulated; and indeed they want new categories of legal service providers to be regulated as well.)

In England and Wales, the call of these campaigners was answered in 2004, with the publication of an independent review, now known as the Clementi Report. Sir David Clementi (an accountant and not a lawyer) had been appointed by the Lord Chancellor to review the regulatory framework for legal services. Meeting and responding to concerns about restrictive practices in the legal marketplace, he recommended considerable liberalization. This led directly to the Legal Services Act 2007 which, amongst many other provisions, permits the setting up of new types of legal businesses called 'alternative business structures' (ABSs), so that non-lawyers can own and run legal businesses; it allows external investment, such as private equity or venture capital, to be injected into legal businesses by outside investors; and it lets non-lawyers become partners in law firms. (In Scotland, incidentally, there is similar but more conservative legislation.)

As I write, in May 2012, this story is still unfolding in England and Wales. In October 2011, the new ownership rules came into force. Since then, bold announcements have been made. It has been reported that one leading national firm, Irwin Mitchell, aims to be the first UK firm to float on the Stock Exchange. The world's first listed law firm, Australia's Slater & Gordon, has acquired an English personal injury law firm (licensed as an ABS) for a figure in excess of £50 million. At the same time, many other law firms are vying in talks with private equity houses for the £1 billion that RBS estimates is available for external investment in firms when they become ABSs. And to give a taste of what external investment might achieve, the private equity-backed group of law firms, QualitySolictors—whose members have concessions in many of the stores of retail giant WH Smith—has launched a multi-million pound series of peak-time TV advertisements.

Meanwhile, the licensing of ABSs by the Solicitors Regulation Authority began in March 2012. The first major consumer brand to be granted ABS status was The Co-operative Legal Services, part of the Co-operative Group. Licensed to engage in three reserved legal activities—probate, conveyancing, and litigation— the Co-op has announced plans to provide legal services from its 330 UK bank branches and intends to create 3,000 new jobs in the legal sector.

These kinds of development are of profound significance and represent a major departure from conventional legal services. Not all of the moves were triggered directly by the Legal Services Act but this legislation—and here is the key point rather than the details of particular initiatives—is engendering a remarkable and unprecedented entrepreneurial spirit in the legal market in the UK. Even where there is not formal liberalization, we are seeing a liberation from the constraints of narrow thinking about the way in which legal services can be delivered. No one knows where this will lead us. It is too early for authoritative pronouncements about the precise outcomes. That is the nature of the market. All we can be sure of, I believe, is that major change is upon us.

Investors, entrepreneurs, and High Street brands together are recognizing that the UK's £25 billion legal market is far from efficient and there are great opportunities for offering legal services in new, less costly, more client-friendly ways. These new players are not committed to traditional ways of working. They do not believe, for example, that all legal work need be undertaken by expensive lawyers working in expensive buildings in expensive city centres. They do not insist, as so many traditional lawyers still maintain, that legal work is best undertaken on an hourly billing basis. They are not constrained by old ways of working. They are passionate about change, and they are often better business managers than most lawyers who tend to have had little training in the actual running of commercial concerns. How different the legal world will surely be when influenced over time by the retail industry, by the management methods of corporate boards, and with the backing of venture capital and private equity.

In short, market forces are sweeping through the legal profession in the UK and these will bring intense new competitive pressures for traditional law firms. The extent of the impact of liberalization is a matter of considerable current debate. Many major law firms, for example, maintain that all of this is of relevance and threat only to High Street law firms which undertake high-volume, low-margin work (that is, large quantities of legal work of modest value). They say, for example, that they have no need for external investment. However, they should bear in mind that liberalization will help to entice the 'Big 4' accounting firms to return to the legal market (see Chapter 12) with all the competition that this will bring. Also, the large firms may not need extra cash to continue practising as they have in the past but it is not clear that they can comfortably afford to back new service opportunities, such as setting up shared services centres for major clients (see Chapter 2).

Lawyers in countries yet to have been liberalized (which is most countries) will often dismiss the phenomenon of liberalization for a different reason—they regard this as a quirk of a small number of misguided jurisdictions. I anticipate, however, that when this liberalization gives rise to legal businesses and legal services that better meet clients' growing more-for-less challenge, then this will have a ripple effect around the world. General Counsel of global businesses who benefit from new forms of service in liberalized regimes will not unreasonably ask for similar service in their own countries. Law firms in traditional markets may find themselves at a competitive disadvantage, unable to raise funds for ambitious new ventures, for example. Of course, whether and how other jurisdictions formally respond to the possibility of liberalization remains to be seen. In the US, many related questions are under deep scrutiny by the American Bar Association's 20/20 Commission, while a similar initiative is likely to be launched shortly in Canada. I predict that within ten years or so, after intense agonizing and various changes of direction, most major jurisdictions in the West and many emerging jurisdictions too will have liberalized in the manner of England. And, even if they do not, liberalization in some countries will bring liberation in most others.

Information Technology

Much of my work over the past 30 years has been devoted to thinking and writing about the impact of information technology on lawyers and the courts. I have also advised innumerable law firms, in-house departments, and governments on this same subject. The legal profession has not generally been swift to embrace new systems but it is increasingly finding it impossible to avoid the technology tidal wave.

IT is now pervasive in our world. There are over 2.2 billion Internet users, 800 million subscribers to Facebook, 3.5 billion email accounts, 1 million kilometres of sub-sea fibre-optic cables, more than 5 billion subscriptions to mobile phones, and, every two days, according to Google's Eric Schmidt, 'we create as much information as we did from the dawn of civilisation up until 2003'. Every two days, in fact, we create more than 5 quintillion (5×10^{18}) bytes of data. IT and the Internet are not passing fads. On the contrary, courtesy of cloud computing, information and processing power are increasingly being made available as a utility, in the manner of water and electricity.

And yet, many lawyers, in an untutored way, tell me that IT is over-hyped. They point to the bursting of the dotcom bubble and claim—based on who knows what—that the impact of technology is slowing down. This is grotesquely to misunderstand the trend. A few lawyers have heard of Moore's Law: not a law of the land, but a prediction made in 1965 by Gordon Moore, the man who founded Intel. He projected then that every two years or so the processing power of computers would double, and yet its cost would halve. Sceptics at the time claimed that this trend would last for a few years and no more. In the event, it is still going strong and computer scientists and material scientists say that it is likely to continue unabated for the foreseeable future.

In his formidable book, *The Singularity is Near*, Ray Kurzweil gives a practical illustration of the future consequences of Moore's Law, if it continues to hold. By 2020, we are told, the average desktop computer will have the same processing power as the human brain, which neuroscientists tell us is approximately 10^{16} calculations per second. I find it amazing that in 1973, when I was 12, I held in my hand my first (large) electronic calculator, and that in less than 50 years a machine of the same size will have the same processing power as the human brain. But this is not nearly as remarkable as the following—that by 2050, according to Kurzweil, the average desktop machine will have more processing power than all of humanity combined. You can call me radical, but it seems to me that if we can see the day in which the average desktop machine has more processing power than all of humanity combined, then it might be time for lawyers to rethink some of their working practices. It is simply inconceivable that information technology will radically alter all corners of our economy and society and yet somehow legal work will be exempt from any change.

Note too that this (literally) exponential growth in processing power is mirrored in most other aspects of technology (from the number of transistors on a chip, to hard disk capacity, to computer memory, to the number of websites, and more). But the nature and role of technology is also changing. We have moved firmly into the era of Web 2.0, which basically means that ordinary human beings (not computer specialists) can contribute and participate directly on the Web. If you were a user of the Web in 1997 (when there were around 40 or 50 million users) you would have been the passive recipient of whatever information website providers chose to publish or broadcast in your direction. Today, users are becoming providers. Readers are authors. Recipients are now participants. Users can contribute. We are finding radically new ways to produce information and to collaborate with one another, whether as bloggers, users of social networks, or contributors to shared, online resources such as Wikipedia and YouTube.

It is exciting and yet disconcerting to contemplate that there is no finishing line for IT and the Internet. Aside from the ongoing and radical changes in the underlying and enabling technologies, innumerable new applications emerge on a daily basis. It is bizarre to think that in, say, two or three years' time, our online lives will be dominated by systems that very few of us have heard of today, or indeed that may not yet have been devised. Three years ago, hardly any lawyers had heard of Twitter. Today, more than 300 million people are users. And yet, even with that number of subscribers, I always get the sense that lawyers are waiting for Twitter to take off. In resisting Twitter and other emerging systems, what we are often witnessing is a phenomenon that I call 'irrational rejectionism'—the dogmatic and visceral dismissal of a technology with which the sceptic has no direct personal experience. One key challenge for the legal profession, however, is to adopt new systems earlier; to identify and grasp the opportunities afforded by emerging technologies.

We need, as lawyers, to be open-minded because we are living in an era of unprecedented technological change. Consider recent progress in artificial intelligence (AI) and, in particular, the achievements of Watson, IBM's AI-based system that competed—in a live broadcast in 2011—on the US television general knowledge quiz show *Jeopardy!* Watson beat the show's two finest ever human contestants. This is a phenomenal technological feat, combining advanced natural language understanding, machine learning, information retrieval, knowledge processing, speech synthesis, and more. While the remarkable Google retrieves information for us that might be relevant, Watson shows how AI-based systems, in years to come, will actually speak with us and solve our problems.

It is significant that many new and emerging applications do not simply computerize and streamline pre-existing and inefficient manual processes. Rather than *automate*, many systems *innovate*, which, in my terms, means they allow us to perform tasks that previously were not possible (or even imaginable). There is a profound message here for lawyers—when thinking about IT and the Internet, the challenge is not just to automate current working practices that are not efficient. The challenge is to innovate, to practise law in ways that we could not have done in the past.

At the same time, though, many of these innovative technologies are disruptive. This means they do not support and sit happily alongside traditional ways of working. Instead they fundamentally challenge and change conventional habits. And so it will be in law. These pervasive, exponentially growing, innovative technologies will come to disrupt and radically transform the way lawyers and courts operate.

Many of the changes brought by technology, and especially by Web 2.0, should be familiar to younger members of the legal profession, as full-fledged members of the Internet generation (which I define as those people who cannot remember a pre-Internet world). Interestingly, though, most young lawyers have not yet made the connection between their social use of information technology and its introduction and potential in their working lives.

In summary, then, I am suggesting that the more-for-less challenge, liberalization, and information technology will together drive immense and irreversible change in the way that lawyers work. There is something of a perfect storm here. Liberalization and information technology on their own would bring (and enable) reform but it is the more-for-less challenge, this imperative driven by grim economic conditions, that is and will continue to be the dominant force.

2 | Strategies for Success

The three drivers of change are urging law firm leaders around the world to contemplate opportunities and threats that the legal market has had little reason to confront in the past. With clients under cost pressures and the business environment changing rapidly, prudent law firms everywhere are trying to develop compelling responses to the new market conditions. In other words, law firms are spending much time and effort in thinking through their strategies for the next few years and beyond.

Charging Less

It might be thought that the best way to meet the more-for-less challenge would be for law firms simply to charge less. For businesses that enjoyed almost uninterrupted yearly growth in profit and turnover for the 20 years leading up to 2007, the suggestion of charging less is not normally greeted with unbridled enthusiasm. Nonetheless, law firms, in these difficult times, like to show willing and so many have recently been proposing 'alternative fee arrangements' (sometimes known as AFAs) to their clients.

The 'alternative' that lawyers have in mind is to 'hourly billing' which has been the dominant way of charging for legal services since the mid-1970s. In truth, hourly billing is not simply a way of pricing and billing legal work; it is a mindset and a way of life. Lawyers charge for their time—for their input and not their output. And, until not long ago, most clients have seemed comfortable with this approach.

The shortcomings of hourly billing are well illustrated by an anecdote involving my daughter. When she was 12, she asked me for a summer job. I needed some administrative work carried out and she agreed to take on the task. She asked me how much I intended to pay her and I responded, unreflectively, that I thought I would pay her a certain amount per hour. She thought about that for a few seconds, smiled, and then said, 'Well, I'll take my time then.' If a 12-year-old can see the shortcomings of hourly billing, then it puzzles me that major international corporations cannot also see the problem here. Hourly billing is an institutionalized disincentive to efficiency. It rewards lawyers who take longer to complete tasks than their more organized colleagues, and it penalizes legal advisers who operate swiftly and efficiently. All too often, the number of hours spent by a law firm bears little relation to the value that is brought. A junior lawyer who expends 50 hours on a task can sometimes provide much less value than half-an-hour of the work of a seasoned practitioner (drawing on his or her lifetime of experience).

The dominant culture in so many major commercial firms, however, is for lawyers to churn out as many chargeable hours as possible. Underlying this practice is a business model for professional firms that has ruled for several decades—the ideal, in theory and practice, is to have a pyramidic structure at the top of which is the equity partner (the owner) of a law firm, beneath whom are junior lawyers whose efforts bring far more revenue to the firm than they are paid as salary. On this model, the broader the base of the pyramid, the more profitable is the firm. And so, in major US firms, for example, many associates are expected to work between 2,000 and 2,500 chargeable hours each year, a set-up that ensures great profitability for law firms but one with which clients are increasingly disillusioned.

In passing, I might add a word or two about rates and incomes. In those large commercial firms where partners' hourly rates exceed, say, £750 per hour and their associates' charges are about half of this, this yields very significant profits for these partners. There are over 50 firms in the world in which many of the partners earn over £1 million per year and, in some, their take is much greater than this. Many of these partners confess that when they entered the law they never dreamt of such incomes and that they had not chosen the law as a career because it would be well remunerated. In contrast, many high-powered law graduates today enter the law precisely because of the promise of considerable wealth. They may be disappointed. Although a handful of these global practices are likely to continue earning very substantial incomes, it may well be that the golden era for many law firms has passed. The more-for-less challenge will drive down profitability.

The scales of income just mentioned understandably give rise to media and public characterization of lawyers as 'fat cats'. However, the overwhelming majority of lawyers around the world earn much more modestly. In most large jurisdictions, approximately 40 per cent of the law firms are run by sole practitioners and about 75 per cent have four partners or fewer. In these practices, the profits are considerably lower, in line with senior public sector workers rather than private bankers.

Alternative Fee Arrangements

Returning to the vexed issue of charging, many law firms, as said, have sought recently to meet clients' demands for lower fees by proposing methods of charging that are not time-based. There has been an upsurge of proposals for work being undertaken on a fixed-cost basis or on a capped basis (where an upper limit to the fees is agreed). Others have gone further and put forward more exotic approaches such as 'value billing', which involves, in a variety of ways, charging for the value of the work undertaken rather than the time expended; or, a variant on this, charging for time and cost saved rather than time spent.

These proposals have generally been prompted by in-house lawyers who, under cost pressures, have formally invited law firms to submit 'new' or 'innovative' suggestions for the pricing of their services. These requests have often been made as part of a broader process of selection of what are known as 'panels' of law firms. A panel, essentially, is a group of preferred firms. The selection process is quite formal, undertaken through byzantine documents, entitled RFPs (requests for proposals) or ITTs (invitations to tender). Increasingly, in-house lawyers have also been working alongside, or been displaced by, professional procurement people who are more experienced in driving down the cost of external suppliers.

There is much to be said both for and against these panels and procurement professionals, but, for now, the crucial point to grasp is that this competitive tendering process does not seem to be yielding the savings that clients require. Alternative fee arrangements seem to be failing to deliver significant savings for clients for at least two reasons. The first is that most AFAs are derived from hourly billing thinking—in calculating fixed fees, for example, the starting point of many law firms is the amount that would have been charged on a conventional, hourly billing basis. Fixed fees, therefore, often represent but a slight variation on hourly billing. Second, and more importantly, very few firms when proposing AFAs do so with the intention of becoming less profitable; and so, if they do not propose to change the way they work (and rarely do they), then the alternative fee proposal is often little more than a repackaging of the original (too costly) proposition. The feedback I am hearing and the private research I have examined suggest that competitive tendering and the resulting proposals of alternative fee arrangements are delivering to clients an overall reduction in the cost of legal services of about 10 per cent. Whether they are major organizations or consumers, the harsh reality for clients who need to slash their legal budgets in half is that pricing differently will not be sufficient to meet their more-for-less challenge. I believe it is now necessary to move from pricing differently to working differently.

The Two Winning Strategies

In my view, there are only two viable strategies available to the legal world to help it cope with the more-for-less challenge. I call these the efficiency strategy and the collaboration strategy. In short, the efficiency strategy maintains that we must find ways of cutting the costs of legal service, while the collaboration strategy suggests that clients should come together and share the costs of certain forms of legal service. The efficiency strategy is likely to be favoured over the next few years, whereas the collaboration strategy will come to dominate in the longer term.

Many law firm leaders, when they hear me speak of the efficiency strategy, agree immediately that legal costs need to be reduced. They may then go on to discuss how their overheads should be trimmed, often by spending less on back-office functions such as technology, marketing, and human resources. It may be that such measures are appropriate in running a leaner machine, but these are not the cost reductions to which I am referring when I advocate the efficiency strategy. Instead, my claim is that the cost of lawyering itself has become too high. Most clients tell me that they do not mind paying significant rates for experienced lawyers but they do object, with increasing indignation, to paying, for example, high hourly rates for relatively junior lawyers to undertake what they perceive as routine and repetitive work. This is the crux of the matter.

In every legal business I visit or advise, I find significant amounts of work being undertaken by young lawyers that is administrative or process-based. The work requires more process than judgement, procedure instead of strategy or creativity. Examples are document review in litigation, due diligence work, basic contract drafting, and rudimentary legal research. Here is the great opportunity for change. It is to identify work that can be routinized and undertaken more efficiently, whether by less qualified, lower-cost human beings, or through computerization. This leads us naturally down a path towards the 'commoditization' of legal work (see Chapter 3) and to what I have termed the 'decomposing' and 'multi-sourcing' of legal work (Chapter 4). These are not fanciful theoretical notions. They are a principal preoccupation of most of the in-house lawyers with whom I meet and of many law firm leaders too.

As for the collaboration strategy, this is more radical and, at first sight for many lawyers, may seem implausible. The idea, once more, is that to meet the more-for-less challenge, clients can and will come together and share the costs of certain types of legal service. This strategy can be pursued in conjunction with, or instead of, implementing the efficiency strategy.

The most dramatic example of the collaboration strategy is one I have advocated for some time for major banks. It applies to their work in regulatory compliance. Major banks spend many hundreds of millions of pounds each year on compliance. Many of these financial institutions operate in well over 100 countries, each with different legislation and regulations, and each requiring not only compliance with their respective rules but also regular submissions of documentation and forms to their regulatory bodies. Keeping up to date with new regulation and changes in old regulation, educating tens of thousands of people on their obligations, understanding the local practices and preferences of regulators, introducing standard processes for supporting the preparation and submission of documentation—these are the tasks facing compliance specialists.

My simple contention is that some banks could come together and share the costs of undertaking many of the compliance jobs that they have in common. This would not be appropriate, of course, for compliance tasks that are sensitive, confidential, or competitive; but much compliance work is administrative and non-competitive and the duplication of effort across the banking

world is massive and unnecessarily costly. My suggestion, therefore, is that banks club together and set up, for example, shared
services centres, which would help them to undertake at least
some compliance activities at vastly reduced cost. For law firms
which benefit from advising each bank in turn on their compliance work, this 'compliance process outsourcing' (as I call it)
would be a grave development. No longer would they be able to
recycle much of their work across their various clients. Instead,
clients would collaborate with a smaller number of firms. I expect
that one or two law firms would enjoy great commercial success
if directly involved in supporting the collaborating banks. But,
for other firms, this could be very threatening for their banking
departments.

Clients can also collaborate in the development of systems. A
case study here is Rulefinder, an online legal risk management
tool developed by one of my clients, the international law firm
Allen & Overy. This service offers help with the rules and practices relating to international shareholding disclosure. This is a
complex and frequently changing area of regulation that affects all
major financial institutions. Innovatively, six leading banks came
together and collaborated with Allen & Overy and so shared the
costs of producing the system.

But the collaboration strategy is not just for large financial institutions. In England, for example, the in-house legal departments
of a number of local authorities have convened over the last few
years and in a similar way are sharing the costs of common legal
work. This philosophy could equally extend to small businesses
and individuals—new-look legal businesses will no doubt spring
up to serve communities of legal users rather than individuals or
organizations on their own.

3 | Commoditizing the Law

Central to the efficiency and collaboration strategies, as introduced in the previous chapter, and also to the general idea of working differently, is a term that is vile and yet vital—that of 'commoditization'. This has become a rather overused notion in the legal world and, unhelpfully, it is a word that is often bandied about with little precision. When many lawyers speak of commoditization, they are prone to do so in bleak and dismissive terms—commoditized legal work, it is intoned with deep regret, is work from which we can no longer make money. The thrust here is that work that was once handcrafted can now be routinized and disposed of quickly with little need for lawyers' intervention. In contrast, from the client's point of view, this shift towards routinization is a good thing, because it attracts much lower fees.

A False Dichotomy

Commoditized legal work (loosely so called) is often distinguished from what I term 'bespoke' legal work. I have used the word 'bespoke' for many years but have come to realize that, beyond England, it sometimes requires some explanation. Think about clothing for a moment. A bespoke suit is an outfit that has been customized, made to measure, and tailored for the precise contours and topography of its owner. It is handmade, handcrafted, and cut specifically for one individual alone. By analogy, I believe that many lawyers regard legal work as highly bespoke. Their client's circumstances are unique and each requires the handcrafting or fashioning of a solution, honed specifically for the individual matter at issue. This is the conception of legal problem-solving that is impressed upon law students in many law schools, where it seems that all problems put before them have features so distinctive that they could require the attention of the Supreme Court. It is also a model of legal services that is found in our literature and theatre, when lawyers look assiduously for smoking guns or loopholes.

I take the view that regarding legal work as bespoke in nature is an unhelpful—if often romantic—fiction. I accept that some legal issues that arise do call for the application of acute legal minds and the handcrafting of tailored solutions. But I believe much less legal work requires bespoke treatment than many lawyers would have their clients believe. More than this, I contend that deploying bespoke techniques in many instances is to adopt cottage-industry methods when mass production and mass customization techniques are now available to support the delivery of a less costly and yet better service.

A further source of confusion here is the oversimplification in thinking which concludes that work is either bespoke or in some vague sense commoditized. This dichotomy urges many lawyers to insist that if they are to avoid non-profitable commoditized work, they must then focus only on bespoke endeavour. They believe these are the only two options.

The Evolution of Legal Service

I maintain that this binary distinction between bespoke and com-moditized legal work is a false dichotomy and that legal services are in fact evolving through five different stages which I call bespoke, standardized, systematized, packaged, and commod-itized, as depicted in Figure 3.1.

In practice, most good practitioners do not undertake much of their work in a bespoke manner. To be sure, and I want to stress this, difficult problems do arise that undoubtedly require bespoke atten-tion; but, far more frequently, lawyers are asked to tackle problems which bear a strong similarity to those they have faced in the past. Indeed, one of the reasons clients select one lawyer over another, or one firm over another, is precisely that they believe that the lawyer or firm has undertaken similar work previously. Most clients would be horrified to think, especially if they are being billed on an hourly basis, that each new piece of work they pass to law firms is set about with a fresh sheet of paper and embarked upon from scratch. On the contrary, clients expect a degree of standardization.

Take an employment contract as an example. If a bespoke approach were adopted, each employment agreement would be

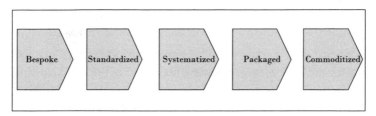

FIGURE 3.1 The evolution of legal service

drafted afresh, starting with a blank canvas. However, unless the circumstances of the employment arrangement were particularly unusual, informed clients would expect standardization in two forms. First, they would imagine some form of standard process would be in play—perhaps a checklist or a procedure manual. Second, they would anticipate that their lawyers would use some kind of standard template or precedent as a starting point. In most reputable law firms, this kind of standardization, both of process and substance, is widely embraced. Clients have no interest in paying for the re-invention of the wheel. ✓

But the evolution of legal service does not stop at standardization. With the advent of information technology, a further step can be taken—that of systematization. This can extend to the computerization of checklists or procedure manuals into what are known as workflow systems. These are commonly used in the insurance industry where there is automation of high-volume, often low-value, tasks and activities. Where there are many tasks, activities, and people involved, and yet the process can be proceduralized, automated workflow can greatly enhance the efficiency of legal work. Systematization can also extend, however, to the actual drafting of documents. To use the employment contract example again, automated document assembly is a technique that requires users to answer a series of questions on screen (for example, the name of the employee, the starting date of employment, salary, and so forth) and after completion of an online form, a relatively polished first draft is compiled and emerges. The underlying technology for this has been in existence since the early 1980s—it is a kind of rule-based decision tree, so that answers to particular questions cause a paragraph or sentence or word to be inserted or deleted, as the case may be. Automated document assembly or production tends to have the added advantage that the user answering the questions need not be a legal expert or even a lawyer.

I know of one firm that systematized its document drafting internally and claimed that this new efficiency was a key differentiator for them in the market. However, one savvy client perceptively inquired: if drafting employment contracts, at least for the majority of employees, involves no more than completing a form online, then why can this not be done directly by the human resources department within the client organization? This line of thinking leads naturally to the 'packaging' of legal services. It occurs when lawyers pre-package and make their experience available to clients on an online basis. It offers an entirely new way of tapping into lawyers' expertise, under a form of licensing arrangement. For the client, this can mean dramatically lower costs of service, while for the law firm it offers the opportunity for them to make money while they sleep—it is a radical departure from the hourly billing model, because the lawyers' expertise is used without any direct consumption of their time.

My longest-standing client is the tax practice of Deloitte. Over the past decade, they have progressed along a similar evolutionary path in respect of their tax compliance work: helping clients to prepare and submit their corporate tax returns. In the beginning, this was a handcrafted activity but they have moved steadily along the spectrum and, in the UK, they distilled the collective expertise of around 250 of their tax specialists into a system for clients to use directly. In packaging their tax knowledge in this way, they fundamentally changed their business model. They created a service that they intended would be of lower cost to clients and, because they have so many users, more profitable for Deloitte than the traditional bespoke offering.

From the client's point of view the arguments in favour of moving from left to right on my evolutionary path are compelling—as we move from left to right, the cost of legal service comes down, the price becomes more certain, the time taken to complete work reduces, and the quality—surprisingly for some—goes up (the collective expertise of many professionals invariably outclasses even the most talented bespoke performance).

Many lawyers respond dismissively to the idea of packaging legal services. They say that they did not go to law school to package their knowledge, they are not publishers, and they are certainly not software engineers. I look at the world very differently. I think if we can find new, cheaper, more convenient, and less forbidding ways of delivering legal services, then we should be adapting the way we work and adopting these new techniques. Our focus should be on helping our clients to meet their formidable more-for-less challenge rather than obstinately holding on to outdated, inefficient working practices.

I do suggest that some legal work will evolve yet further and become commoditized, by which I mean readily available at no or low cost on the Internet, as a form of online legal service (see Chapter 9). Whereas many lawyers confuse standardization with commoditization, I believe the latter is most usefully confined to referring to legal work that is so commonplace and routinizable that it can be made available, in open-source spirit, on the Web. I acknowledge that lawyers will not benefit commercially from the commoditization of legal services in this sense, but I urge that commoditization will be fundamental in radically increasing access to justice for those who cannot currently afford legal services.

4 | Working Differently

I am anxious to add one point of clarification to my discussion of the evolution of legal services in the previous chapter. What I am *not* saying is that for any piece of legal work—say, a deal or dispute—the question that arises is: in which of my five boxes does that legal matter sit? I am saying something subtler than this, namely, that for any deal or dispute, no matter how small or large, it is possible to break it down, to 'decompose' the work, into a set of constituent tasks. And it is in respect of each of these tasks, not the job as a whole, that one can ask: what is the most efficient way of undertaking this work, and to which of the five boxes should the tasks be allocated?

If my first major point in this book is that the legal market faces the more-for-less challenge, then my second is that legal work can be decomposed and sourced in new and different ways.

Decomposing

Legal engagements such as deals and disputes, I am saying, are not monolithic, indivisible professional engagements that must all be sourced and undertaken in one way. Instead we can decompose (economists would say 'disaggregate') work into various tasks and should undertake each, I propose, in as efficient a manner as possible. None of what I say is to betray quality. Rather, my claim is that there are ways of undertaking individual legal tasks that will deliver quality as high as conventional legal service (and sometimes even higher) but at far lower cost.

When I speak at conferences about decomposing legal work I am often met afterwards by a lawyer who will, quite amicably, tell me that he enjoyed my remarks and agrees that the legal world is in need of a considerable shake-up. He will go further and concede that what I say about commoditization and decomposition applies to every area of legal practice... except one. And the lawyer will then tell me why it is that what I say about working differently does not apply to his own area of legal work. Particularly insistent are litigators who will maintain that every dispute is unique and that there is no scope for decomposing and the rest. This reflected my experience of the 1990s, when I worked for many years with a leading firm of litigators (Masons, now Pinsent Masons). It was true, at that time, that dispute work was not decomposed and it was common, for the large construction and technology disputes in which we specialized, for almost all aspects of the work to be handed over to the firm in their entirety. However, I have since come to see that not all of the tasks that we and other firms then undertook are any longer best discharged by law firms. And so to the sceptics by way of demonstration, I suggest that the conduct of litigation can be divided into the nine tasks that are laid out in Table 4.1. I am not suggesting that this is the only way of decomposing litigation but I hope it gives a flavour of my approach.

TABLE 4.1. Litigation, decomposed

document review
legal research
project management
litigation support
(electronic) disclosure
strategy
tactics
negotiation
advocacy

Over the past few years, the question I have been asking litigators in the finest of the world's law firms is this: which of these nine tasks are you *uniquely* qualified to undertake? In the UK, the answer to this query has invariably been 'two' tasks (strategy and tactics) and, in the US, the answer has tended to be 'three' (strategy, tactics, and advocacy). And for these two or three tasks, clients will continue to want the direct advice and guidance of skilled lawyers. However, I am increasingly hearing from General Counsel that alternative providers can now take on the remaining tasks at lower cost and to a higher quality than traditional law firms.

Take, for example, document review. In the past, junior lawyers were deployed by law firms, at significant hourly rates, to work through large bodies of documents (sometimes many millions of them), often simply to index them or to impose some very basic legal classification. Document review can now be outsourced to third party specialist providers, in low-cost countries such as India, and undertaken to a higher quality for around one-seventh of the cost.

Consider a further illustration, that of project management. Many litigators confide in me that they are no longer lawyers;

they are now project managers. I sometimes inquire about the extent of their training in project management and am often told, with a straight face, that they went on a two-day training course three years previously. I tend to quip in response that if a project manager said to a lawyer that he or she was now a lawyer, having undertaken a three-day training course in the law, that project manager would be dismissed as misguided. Project management is a significant discipline in its own right, with its own techniques, methods, systems, and degree courses. When I look inside major accounting firms, consulting practices, and construction companies, I find sophisticated project management. In law firms, on the other hand, project management seems to involve little more than buying some new lever-arch files and cracking open a new pack of yellow stickers. It is our collective arrogance as lawyers that we feel we can take on a neighbouring discipline over a weekend. We cannot. And clients now recognize that they will find the best project managers not in law firms but within other providers. I passionately believe that project management will be central to the successful conduct of large-scale deals and disputes in the future. But if lawyers are not sufficiently trained in this discipline, competitors from other professions and sectors will undertake this work in their stead.

I can undertake similar analysis of each of the other tasks in litigation for which law firms are no longer uniquely qualified. Many of these tasks are routine and repetitive, largely administrative, and can now be sourced in different ways. Equally, I can subdivide transaction work into an analogous list of tasks, as in Table 4.2 (again not put forward as definitive but included simply to give a taste of what I have in mind).

TABLE 4.2. Transactions, decomposed

due diligence
legal research
transaction management
template selection
negotiation
bespoke drafting
document management
legal advice
risk assessment

Alternative Sourcing and Multi-Sourcing

When I say that pricing differently is not enough and that lawyers must move towards working differently, I have in mind the adoption of one or more alternative ways of sourcing legal work. In the past, when confronted with a legal job, a client had a simple choice: undertake it internally or pass it out to an external law firm (or perhaps a blend of the two). The legal world has changed, so that new alternative sources of legal service are now available. I have identified 15 ways of sourcing legal work, as laid out in Table 4.3.

In this introductory book I can give but a flavour of each.

In-sourcing is when lawyers undertake legal work themselves, using their own internal resources. This could be, for example, when an in-house legal department decides to conduct all of its negotiation and drafting internally, without any external advice or assistance.

De-lawyering is my inelegant term for the process by which a legal task is handed over to a non-lawyer—such as a paralegal or a legal executive—to discharge. Many tasks do not require the

TABLE 4.3. Sources of legal service

in-sourcing
de-lawyering
relocating
off-shoring
outsourcing
subcontracting
co-sourcing
near-shoring
leasing
home-sourcing
open-sourcing
crowd-sourcing
computerizing
solo-sourcing
no-sourcing

expertise and cost of qualified lawyers and can be taken on by other skilled and knowledgeable individuals within the legal sector.

Relocating involves an organization moving some of its legal work to less costly locations, but still within countries in which the main business already has a presence. An illustration here is the US-based international law firm Orrick, which has a global operations centre based in Wheeling, West Virginia.

Off-shoring is the transfer of legal work to countries in which labour and property costs are lower. Many large banks have off-shored some of their legal activities in this way—for example, to India and Malaysia—to places where they have already moved other functions, such as their call centres or their finance functions. On this model, the off-shored legal resource remains part of the bank.

Outsourcing, in contrast, entails the conduct of legal work by a third party provider. This is often referred to as 'legal process outsourcing' or 'LPO'. Routine legal tasks, such as document review, are handed to these specialist support companies, which, again, are usually in low-cost locations.

Subcontracting is an option open to law firms. On this approach, legal work is passed to other (usually smaller) law firms, which carry much lower overheads. Thus, several large London-based law firms subcontract work to English qualified lawyers working in South Africa and New Zealand, while others engage lower-cost regional firms within the UK. Subcontracting can halve the costs of certain legal tasks.

Co-sourcing occurs when organizations collaborate in the delivery of some legal service, often through some shared services facility. Powerful illustrations of this, as noted in Chapter 2, are the cooperation of the in-house legal departments of local authorities in England and the plans of various banks to set up common facilities for the conduct of their compliance work.

Near-shoring is similar to off-shoring but the work is carried out in a neighbouring, low-cost jurisdiction that is in a closer time zone to the law firm or in-house department that is parcelling out the legal tasks. Allen & Overy and Herbert Smith, leading London-headquartered international law firms, have both near-shored by setting up facilities in Belfast, in Northern Ireland, for the disposal of routine legal work.

Leasing is the engagement of lawyers for limited periods and often on a project basis. These lawyers do not belong to conventional law firms. Instead, they are made available through agencies that manage their placement. Axiom is a leading example of a legal leasing agency. Founded in 2000, this business has been growing rapidly, leasing lawyers largely to corporate clients, often to help them to meet peaks in demand. This is particularly useful for in-house departments that downsize, because they will periodically need to boost their own capability and Axiom lawyers are about half the price of those from conventional firms. Significantly, though, two law firms in England have set up similar leasing facilities—Berwin Leighton Paisner (in 2008) with its Lawyers on Demand service and Eversheds (in 2011) with its Agile offering.

Home-sourcing embraces legal talent that is not currently in the mainstream legal workplace and yet is available, often on a part-time basis, from lawyers who choose to work from their own homes. Enabled to a large extent by ever-improving communications technologies, lawyers who work from home (whether on an employed basis or as independents) are able to join and use the networks of law firms and in-house departments with whom they are working. Home-sourcing has proven to work well for parents who wish both to work and to be available for their young children for much of the day.

Open-sourcing is the provision, at no charge, of all sorts of legal materials (standard documents, guidelines, procedures, opinions, case studies, practical experience, and more) on publicly accessible websites. This is likely to be most effective if organized in the form of a wiki (an online resource that any users can edit and add to).

Crowd-sourcing involves harnessing the collective talents of large groups of individuals who make some of their time available to undertake certain categories of legal task. On one approach, for instance, a legal problem might be broadcast to a large, unknown group of volunteers. And these volunteers—the crowd—respond with their proposed legal solutions. In law firms, practitioners often pop their heads around doors and ask colleagues in relation to an issue they are handling, 'Has anyone seen one of these before?' In the future, lawyers and clients will be able to ask similar questions of large bodies of Internet users. A related service, LawPivot, already allows people to ask questions publicly and the answers given by lawyers are then shared with the user base.

Computerizing is a wide category of sourcing which I take to include the three categories of systematizing, packaging, and commoditizing, as introduced in Chapter 3. In general terms, computerization refers to the application of information technology to support or replace some legal tasks, processes, activities, or services.

Solo-sourcing is the engagement of individual specialists, such as law professors or (as is common in England) barristers to conduct specific, decomposed packages of legal work. Illustrations of this are research conducted by academics and opinions written by QCs.

No-sourcing is my final category, and is the option of choosing not to undertake a legal task at all, on the informed view that the task itself is not sufficiently high risk to merit any form of legal sourcing. As an illustration, in-house lawyers often take a view on certain legal portions of legal work and decide that the time and expense that they would require is not commercially justified. They often find this easier to do when work has been decomposed in the manner described earlier in this chapter.

Although each of these 15 techniques, if deployed in isolation, can provide powerful alternative ways of sourcing legal tasks, it is short-sighted to view them as distinct options. My thinking is that, in the future, for any substantial piece of legal work, it will become common practice to decompose the matter in question into manageable tasks, to identify the most efficient way of sourcing each task, and to adopt several of the alternative approaches in combination. This is 'multi-sourcing'. Thus, for a particular deal or dispute, a few if not many sources might contribute to the final product. To achieve this, we may find it useful to apply production-line or manufacturing mentality and methodology to the delivery of legal services: using, for example, just-in-time logistics and global supply chain techniques (underpinned by IT). On this model, one individual organization—a law firm or perhaps a new-look legal business—will likely take over all responsibility for the delivery of the completed, multi-sourced service (as a main contractor will do in a building project).

I am emphatically not advocating some kind of mass production model for legal service. I accept that the circumstances of clients are never identical. But I do not concede that human legal practitioners are needed at all stages across the life cycle of a legal project, even if the final output is tailored. Rather, I regard multi-sourcing and the deployment of IT as leading towards mass customization—using standard processes and systems that can meet the particular needs of clients and yet with a level of efficiency that is akin to that of mass production. A good example is document assembly technology, as described in Chapter 3. An automated drafting system of the kind I describe does not simply print out a single, standard document. Instead, based on a user's answers to specific questions about his or her particular circumstances, the document generated will be one output of countless (often millions of) possible permutations. The end result is a tailored solution, delivered by an advanced system rather than by a human craftsman. That is the future of legal service.

5 | Disruptive Legal Technologies

In management theory, drawing on Clayton Christensen's book, *The Innovator's Dilemma*, a distinction is commonly drawn between sustaining and disruptive technologies. In broad terms, sustaining technologies are those that support and enhance the way that a business or a market currently operates. In contrast, disruptive technologies fundamentally challenge and change the functioning of a firm or a sector. An example of the former category is computerized accounting systems, which sustained and enhanced the work of those who previously laboured over paper ledgers. An illustration of the latter is digital camera technology, which famously disrupted and led in part to the eventual downfall of Kodak, whose business was based on an earlier generation of technology (chemical printing).

Two aspects of disruptive technology theory are noteworthy. First, as the Kodak example illustrates, disruptive technologies can help to unseat and bring about the demise even of market leaders. Second, in the early days of disruptive technologies, market leaders as well as their customers often dismiss the new systems as superficial and unlikely to take off. Later, however, as they gain acceptance, customers often switch quickly to services based on the new technology, whereas providers, unless they are early adopters, are often too late to recognize their real potential and never manage to regain ground.

I claim there are at least 13 disruptive technologies in law (see Table 5.1).

Individually, these existing and emerging systems will challenge and change the way in which certain legal services are delivered. Collectively, they will transform the entire legal landscape. When I refer to disruption I am generally speaking of havoc wreaked on the supply side of the legal market, that is, to law firms and other legal service providers. For the buyer of legal services, this disruption is often very good news indeed. One person's disruption can be another's salvation.

TABLE 5.1. Disruptive legal technologies

automated document assembly
relentless connectivity
electronic legal marketplace
e-learning
online legal guidance
legal open-sourcing
closed legal communities
workflow and project management
embedded legal knowledge
online dispute resolution
intelligent legal search
big data
AI-based problem-solving

In what follows, I offer very brief introductions to each of these disruptive legal technologies.

Automated Document Assembly

These systems, as described in Chapter 3, generate relatively polished and customized first drafts of documents, in response to questions asked of their users. Early work in this field, in the 1980s, was undertaken on systems that could generate wills. Since then, the same technology has been applied in far more ambitious contexts such as the production of loan documentation for large-scale banking transactions. These systems, which can therefore be used within legal businesses or made available online, are disruptive for lawyers who charge for their time, because they enable documents to be generated in minutes whereas, in the past, they would have taken many hours to craft.

Not quite as sophisticated as full-scale automated document assembly systems are those online services that provide users with basic document templates. Consider LegalZoom, a US-based business that makes legal documents available to citizens and businesses who cannot afford lawyers or wish to spend less (and here is the disruption) on their legal issues. LegalZoom has now served over two million customers and its brand is claimed to be better known in the US than that of any law firm. In a similarly disruptive manner, one UK company, Epoq, provides systems and templates that enable banks and insurance companies to provide online services (including document production) to their own clients.

Relentless Connectivity

This refers to systems that together prevent lawyers from entirely disengaging from their clients and the workplace. The technologies include handheld devices, tablets, wireless broadband access, high definition video conferencing, instant messaging, social networking, and email; all bolstered by increasing processing power and storage capacity. When these technologies combine, and the machines (of whatever kind) are switched on, which seems now to be all of the time, the 'presence' of lawyers is increasingly visible to their network of contacts. In turn, clients and colleagues will have and expect to have immediate access to lawyers. This can be disruptive for the working and social lives of lawyers. It is a sobering thought too that we seem destined to become more and not less connected, so that the disruption of relentless connectivity is likely to intensify rather than diminish.

Electronic Legal Marketplace

I use this term to include online reputation systems, which allow clients to share their views, online, on the performance and levels of service of their lawyers (as customers of hotels and restaurants now do); price comparison systems, which put the respective prices and rates of different legal advisers and law firms on simple websites; and online legal auctions, not unlike eBay in concept, but best suited to legal work packages that are routine and repetitive. For lawyers who used to rely on their clients not knowing what alternatives were open to them, these technologies in isolation and together are highly disruptive. Today, these systems—social networks of a sort—are in their early incarnations. In not too many years, they will be as pervasive as the influential printed directories that have ranked lawyers and law firms for the last 20 years or so.

e-Learning

Remarkable progress is being made on the development of online facilities to support legal learning and training. As discussed in Chapter 14, these will challenge and replace most conventional law lectures and, more broadly, will precipitate an overhaul of the traditional methods of law schools generally. The techniques involved extend well beyond online lectures and webinars to the use of simulated legal practice and virtual legal learning environments. Beyond formal education, e-learning will also transform the way that law firms provide and integrate their training and know-how functions. We will see a move from 'just-in-case' classroom training (teaching subjects, just in case the insight provided might be needed in practice at some later stage) to 'just-in-time' learning (interactive, multimedia tools which can supply focused and tailored training on the spot).

Online Legal Guidance

These are systems that can provide legal information, legal guidance, and even legal advice across the Internet. They may or may not be subscription-based. One example is LawHelp in the US, an online resource that helps low- and moderate-income people to find free legal aid programmes in their communities and that answers questions about their legal rights. Another is Probate Wizard, a self-service online facility, supported by guides and videos, which provides users with an easy way of completing the probate process (administrating an estate) in England and Wales. And yet another is MentorLive, RBS's online legal service for businesses, covering employment, health and safety, and environmental law (and incorporating factsheets and report templates).

The threat and disruption to conventional lawyers here is clear: if clients can secure legal guidance and legal documents on an online basis, then this may come to be a low-cost competitor to lawyers whose living is made from traditional, consultative, face-to-face advisory service. And, in the terminology of Chapter 3, if robust and reliable legal help is commoditized and available at no cost to users, then it is hard to imagine, at least in some circumstances, why clients would prefer to pay good money to traditional human advisers.

Legal Open-Sourcing

Consistent with the open-source movement generally, here I envisage sustained online mass collaboration in the field of law—a movement devoted to building up large quantities of public, community-oriented legal materials, such as standard documents, checklists, and flow charts. This is also a form of commoditization (see Chapter 3) and is disruptive for lawyers because, once again, legal content that once was chargeable as part of lawyers' service is now available for no fee. A leading illustration of this phenomenon is the Legal Information

Institute at Cornell University Law School, where, since 1992, they have been publishing law online at no charge and creating materials that help people to understand legal issues. They are sometimes referred to as a leading 'law-not-com' provider of public legal information.

Closed Legal Communities

The idea here is for restricted groups of like-minded lawyers with common interests to come together and collaborate online in private social networks. A cross between LinkedIn and Wikipedia, but solely for the use of small groups of lawyers, the users can build up bodies of collective knowledge and experience. A similar concept in the medical profession has enjoyed considerable success: Sermo, an online community for doctors (no patients or pharmaceutical companies), has over 125,000 users. The best example of this phenomenon in law is Legal OnRamp, described as a collaboration system for in-house counsel, invited outside lawyers, and third party service providers. Lawyers from over 40 countries are already participating, both in the general online community and in private sub-communities that can be set up.

In pursuit of the collaboration strategy described in Chapter 2, in-house lawyers are expressing serious interest in these closed communities—as platforms upon which they might share the costs of certain legal services and also as a tool to encourage and enable closer collaboration amongst their preferred law firms. For firms that are wedded to the notion of servicing their clients separately, this poses a considerable threat.

Workflow and Project Management

For high-volume, repetitive legal work, workflow systems are like automated checklists that drive a standard process from start to finish. Project management systems, on the other hand, are better suited to legal tasks and activities that are more complex, less structured, and yet still amenable to more disciplined handling than the ad hocery that is found in many law firms and in-house departments. For law firms that charge by the hour and so have historically benefited from ineffective case management and inept transaction management, workflow and project management systems represent new efficiencies and, in turn, the prospect of reduced fees.

Embedded Legal Knowledge

In years to come, in many dimensions of our social and working lives, I predict that legal rules will be deeply embedded in our systems and processes. Consider a car that warns its drivers and passengers that the ignition will not work until a built-in breathalysing test is used and passed. This would not require car users to know the precise details of the law and then exercise the option of applying the law. Instead, the law that prohibits driving with excessive alcohol in the bloodstream would be embedded in the car itself. Another example would be an 'intelligent' building that monitors the temperature and other environmental conditions by reference to levels established in health and safety regulations. In the event of some stipulated limit being exceeded, alarms might sound or, in emergency situations, computer screens might even be disabled. Again, this would not require people to know the law and monitor compliance. Rather, the regulations would be embedded in the building. And the building would, as it were, know about its own safety levels and make some decisions accordingly. The disruption here is that, where rules are embedded, lawyers are no longer needed to draw clients' attention to circumstances of legal significance.

Online Dispute Resolution (ODR)

When the process of actually resolving a legal dispute, especially the formulation of the solution, is entirely or largely conducted across the Internet, then we have some form of online dispute resolution (known in the trade as ODR—see Chapter 10 for more detail and some examples). For litigators whose work is premised on the conventional, court-based trial process, ODR, such as e-negotiation and e-mediation, is a challenge to the heart of their business.

Intelligent Legal Search

Emerging systems, if properly primed, are now able, in terms of precision and recall, to outperform paralegals and junior lawyers when reviewing and categorizing large bodies of documents. This is disruptive, not simply for law firms which have profited from employing human beings to wade through roomfuls of paperwork (whether on transactions or dispute-related projects), but also for legal process outsourcers who currently offer similar services. No matter how low human labour costs might be, a system of this kind, once set up, will always be less costly.

Big Data

One of the most exciting current areas of Internet research and practice is the field of 'big data'. The pervasive and worldwide use of information technology and the Internet is spawning unfathomably large datasets, which are too vast and unwieldy to be managed by most conventional tools. A veritable industry of people and systems is now emerging to help to cope with this data challenge; to help us to process and harness its value more effectively. One fascinating result of this work is that big data can yield patterns and correlations that previously we could not have identified. An example is Google Flu Trends—it appears that there is a close relationship between the number of Google search requests on flu-related topics and the number of people who actually have flu. And it seems that by monitoring the use of certain search terms, this enables Google to identify outbreaks of flu earlier and more regularly than when traditional flu-surveillance techniques are deployed.

Very little work has yet been undertaken on the relevance of big data for law. However, I predict that it will prove, in due course, to be of profound significance. For example, by aggregating search data, we might be able to find out what legal issues and concerns are troubling particular communities; by analysing databases of decisions by judges and regulators, we may be able to predict outcomes in entirely novel ways; and by collecting huge bodies of commercial contracts and exchanges of emails, we might gain insight into the greatest legal risks that specific sectors face. The disruption here is that crucial legal insights, correlations, and even algorithms might come to play a central role in legal practice and legal risk management and yet they will not be generated through the work of mainstream lawyers (unless they choose to collaborate with big data scientists).

AI-Based Problem-Solving

If IBM's Watson (an artificially intelligent computer system designed to compete on the US TV quiz show *Jeopardy!*) is able publicly to beat the two finest human competitors, then the days of online problem-solving by computer are not very far away. And when we enter that era, and we apply the same techniques and technologies in law, then we will have AI-based legal problem-solving. This could be an online service that contains vast stores of structured and unstructured legal materials (primary and secondary sources), that can understand legal problems spoken to it in natural language, that can analyse and classify the fact pattern inherent in these problems, that can draw conclusions and offer legal advice, and that can even express this guidance in some computer-simulated voice (in an accent of the user's choosing, perhaps). AI will disrupt not just the world of practising lawyers but also our common perception of the legal process. This is some years away yet but emerging technologies, developing exponentially, may bring artificial intelligence comprehensively to the law sooner than sceptics believe.

PART TWO

The New Landscape

6 | The Future for Law Firms

One central question emerges from the first part of this book: to what extent can lawyers' work be undertaken differently—more quickly, cheaply, and efficiently, but to a higher quality—using alternative methods of working? That is a key question of the day. As noted in Chapter 2, lawyers have for many years performed routine work for which they have been overqualified and for which, in turn, they have been overcharging. In boom times, in what was a sellers' market, there was little need for successful law firms to be detained by the challenge of delivering services in new and more efficient ways. Today, however, as cost pressures from clients intensify, as new service providers emerge, and as new technologies are deployed, it is unwise for any firm to avoid thinking about how it should work differently.

Nonetheless, I find that most traditional practices are not changing much. They are not yet adopting alternative methods of working. This is partly an issue of change management, in that law firms tend to be so busy serving clients and meeting their own financial targets that they allow little time for internal reform—it is not easy to change a wheel on a moving car. It is also, in part, a structural matter, because most law firms still aspire to the old textbook, broad-based pyramidic structure mentioned in Chapter 2; whereas alternative methods of sourcing call for a revision if not rejection of that model. And, if we are honest, there is also reluctance in many firms to believe that they really need to change. There is an inclination, in other words, to cling on to the old ways of working in the hope that there will soon be a solid economic recovery and normal business can be resumed.

Prospects for Law Firms

However, if the analysis and predictions of Part One of this book are sound, then law firms in the coming decade and beyond will be driven relentlessly by their clients to reduce their costs. This is the heart of the more-for-less challenge (see Chapter 1). For most firms, despite their current hesitancy, I predict that this will lead eventually to the deployment and execution of alternative sourcing strategies (Chapter 4). And, in turn, we will witness the end of leverage—at best the pyramid (with partners at the top and less experienced lawyers at the base) will move from being broad-based to narrow-based. No longer will firms aspire to building large teams of junior lawyers as the basis of their profitability. 'To survive', in the memorable words of Theodore Levitt (in his seminal article, 'Marketing Myopia'), lawyers 'will have to plot the obsolescence of what now produces their livelihood'.

In due course, some firms may, for example, choose to strip away their junior and trainee lawyers, or stop recruiting them. They might then operate with a team of high-powered partners, each supported by, say, one associate; and the routine work will be resourced beyond the firm. Others may elect to build their own alternative sourcing capacities, such as internal teams of para-legals, or maybe through the establishment of their own off-shored legal facility. Still others will find opportunities for novel legal services (see Chapter 11), by creating markets that formerly did not exist or by inserting themselves in different places in legal supply chains (for example, by becoming involved far earlier in the life cycles of their clients' business dealings).

Although these changes will impact on all firms (large and small), some larger firms will want to argue that, for 'high-end work', notions such as commoditization, decomposing, and multi-sourcing, are of little relevance. But, on examination, it transpires that this concept of 'high-end work' is something of a myth—even in the world's largest deals and disputes there are substantial components of work that can be routinized and sourced differently. And large firms that insist they only undertake bespoke work, which is a very different claim from asserting that they only do high-end work (bespoke being a subset, often small, of high-end), may find themselves at risk. They may be relegated, for instance, to the role of subcontractor to other organizations that step forward to undertake the project management of sizeable deals and disputes. At the same time, alternative providers may take up the work that these firms previously assigned to their junior lawyers.

A Global Elite?

That said, there may well be a global elite of law firms, around 20 in number today (but likely to merge into a smaller cadre in the coming decade), which feel that they do not need to change. These will be firms which continue to enjoy great commercial success. With some force, they will argue that for bet-the-ranch deals and disputes, clients will still want the services delivered, more or less, as in the past. These firms will say that for really big ticket assignments, there is only a handful of brands that will be tolerated at board level (the 'no one ever got fired for buying IBM' principle) and that, in any event, when the future of an organization is in the balance (whether under threat or in anticipation of a great new venture) legal work is not price sensitive (the 'one million dollars here or there makes no difference in the broader scheme of things' principle). If all of these elite law firms believe this and continue to work as they have in the past, then they may well be right. And it will be hard to convince a group of million-aires that their business model is broken.

However, they should not be overconfident in their belief that, in Levitt's words, 'there is no competitive substitute for the indus-try's major product'. So, if one leading firm breaks rank, or if a major new force (such as a 'Big 4' accounting firm) emerges, and brings a new proposition to the market—a credible brand at half the price of its competitors, for example—then this could funda-mentally and irreversibly change the market; and not just for the elite firms but across the entire profession. Leaders of the elite firms should suspend their likely incredulity at this scenario, if only because major clients, as never before, are commonly saying that they are now actively looking for alternatives to the tradi-tional ways of some of the great firms whom many regard as too costly and sometimes too arrogant.

As for medium-sized firms, to survive and thrive I suspect most will need to merge and seek external investment to enable the changes from their current approach to a new, sustainable, longer-term business model. There is a window of opportunity here—they should recognize that clients' dissatisfaction with some of the leading firms throws up an unprecedented opportunity to be recognized as credible alternatives. To do this, they must find ways of building their reputations, brands, and capabilities.

I believe there will be a market for many years yet for small to medium-sized firms with demonstrable, niche expertise. General Counsel of even the largest of organizations often indicate that they welcome deep expertise and personal service even if offered from modest-sized firms. Usually, it is the talents of a particular lawyer rather than of a particular firm that is the attraction here.

As for much smaller firms with very few partners, aside from those which also offer a genuinely specialist or personal service that some market is prepared to pay for, I find it hard to imagine how these legal businesses will survive in the long run. On the High Street, in liberalized legal regimes, banks and retailers will compete with sole practitioners and small firms for everyday legal services (such as conveyancing, probate, and personal injury work). But it is likely that these alternative business structures, fuelled by external investment and driven by experienced business managers, will standardize, systematize, and package legal services (see Chapter 3) and bring cost savings, efficiencies, and experience that the traditional, small law firms will find impossible to match. This will be the end of lawyers who practise in the manner of a cottage industry. One person who formally reviewed my publication proposal for this book said that they hoped that I would pay more attention than in the past to general purpose small firms. I am afraid I was not inclined to do so, because I do not see much of a future (beyond 2020) for most small firms in liberalized regimes.

What about non - liberalized regimes?

Trial Lawyers and Barristers   ✓

Another group of legal specialists who often maintain that they will be unaffected by economic forces, liberalization, and technology are barristers in England and trial lawyers in law firms around the world.

It is true that much of the work of the oral advocate is highly bespoke in nature and it is not at all obvious how the efforts and expertise of the courtroom lawyer might be standardized or computerized. Indeed, oral advocacy at its finest is probably the quintessential bespoke legal service. I have little doubt, for the foreseeable future, that very high-value and very complex legal issues will continue to be argued before conventional courts in the traditional manner. When there is a life-threatening dispute, clients will continue to secure the talents of the finest legal gladiators who will combat on their behalf. However, it is less clear that instructing barristers or trial lawyers for lower value or less complex disagreements will continue to be regarded as commercially justifiable. Quite apart from a likely shift towards mediation, collaborative lawyering, and other forms of alternative dispute resolution, emerging techniques of dispute containment and dispute avoidance (see Chapter 9) are likely to reduce the number of cases that find final closure in courts of law or even on the steps of the courthouse. Moreover, courtroom appearances themselves will diminish in number with greater uptake of virtual hearings, while online dispute resolution (ODR) will no doubt displace many conventional litigators. The future for truly exceptional senior trial lawyers and barristers looks rosy for some time yet, therefore, but junior civil trial lawyers may need to rethink their futures and prepare to engage in virtual hearings and ODR if they wish to prosper beyond 2020.

In England and Scotland, those barristers and advocates whose practices are devoted to the writing of opinions on complex areas of law will also be less affected by the changes anticipated in this book than most other areas of legal practice, because there is no obvious alternative source for this genuinely bespoke work.

Questions Asked by New Partners

In the context of great change and disruption within law firms, I notice that recently appointed partners of law firms are currently disconcerted and nervous.

In the past, I have found young partners to be an interesting breed. Often in their mid-30s, these bright young lawyers have great energy and considerable experience, but have tended to operate on the expectation that the firms of which they are now part-owners are likely to function and profit in the future much as they have in the past. They have tended to be a confident bunch, pumped up by recent admittance into partnership by their seniors, and satisfied that the effort they have expended has been justified; although they have often been unnerved to discover that becoming a partner is of itself a new beginning and to find themselves on the bottom rung of yet another ladder.

In the past few years, however, I have noted that junior partners are less confident in their position and worry very deeply about the future of the firms they have joined. When I addressed law firms' induction courses for new partners between 1996 and 2006, I felt them dismissive of my seemingly outlandish ideas. Most preferred to look at their BlackBerry devices or draft documents during my presentations. This has changed radically. Today junior partners are all ears, consistently asking me the same set of questions, and are anxious to hear my views. Here are these questions, along with the replies I usually give.

Is our firm viable and sustainable?

The changes I anticipate in Part One of this book are not coming in the next three to six months but they will begin to take hold in the next three to six years. If firms do not embrace alternative sourcing strategies, I doubt the majority will be viable or sustainable in the long term.

Is the business model broken?

Insofar as this refers to the broad-based pyramid with the partner at the top and junior lawyers undertaking routine work at the bottom, then, again within the time scales just noted, I think this model will indeed be broken. Leverage will be replaced by alternative sourcing.

Have the glory years passed?

For many firms, I believe their peak was around 2006. This is not simply a matter of profitability and turnover, for many have improved these since, but a question of the ease with which work is won, the level of fees that clients can be charged without challenge, and the amount of human effort expended. Some elite firms and entrepreneurial firms will go on to enjoy yet greater times, but for many firms, unless they change radically, the glory years have indeed passed.

Are our fixed costs too high?

In the coming years, firms will need to revisit their property strategies, because high rentals in expensive cities will be a costly indulgence in an increasingly networked world with pervasive video links; and the labour costs of large numbers of junior lawyers will also be excessive, largely because of the availability of alternative sourcing in lower-cost regions or countries.

What are we inheriting?

Most junior partners are inheriting outdated, outmoded, low-tech businesses that will soon not be fit for purpose. This means not that there is a lack of great intelligence or talent within the businesses but that the way in which this talent is taken to market is no longer competitively arranged and priced.

Do senior partners care about the long term?

This is a vital question. Regrettably, most law firm leaders that I meet have only a few years left to serve and hope they can hold out until retirement before much that I predict engulfs them. Operating as managers rather than leaders, they are more focused on short-term profitability than long-term strategic health. For junior partners this is tragic because any major re-invention and re-engineering of law firms has to be driven from the top. I find a great contrast here with the large accounting firms, where senior partners seem far more concerned about the prospects of their junior partners. Their philosophy—to regard themselves as temporary custodians of long-term and enduring businesses rather than short-term investors who want to bail out when the price is right—is one than could fruitfully be assumed by more equity partners in law firms.

In other words, it is time for senior partners to think more deeply about a more generous legacy for their successors.

7 | The Shifting Role of In-House Lawyers

Some of the most fulfilled lawyers that I meet work in-house. This means they belong to legal departments that sit within large organizations. Some of these departments—for example, in large banks and corporations—can be very large, with as many as 1,000 lawyers. A career as an in-house lawyer attracts those who want to be at the heart of the organizations that they advise. If you work in a law firm, you are at one remove from the business of your clients. If you work in-house, you are part of the business. Most law students, when contemplating their future careers, tend to imagine themselves working in law firms (other than in the US, where many law students aspire to being government lawyers). In many law schools, there is little formal discussion of the role of in-house lawyers, which is bizarre because these clients are likely to have an enormous influence on the future of legal services.

Legal Risk Management

Most General Counsel (GCs), the leaders of in-house legal teams, tell me that their principal job should be that of managing risk;

that 'legal risk management' should be the core competence and service of in-house lawyers. They often contrast this with what they actually do, which is fight fires—in-house lawyers are faced, on a daily basis, with a barrage of requests, problems, and questions from across their organizations. And they usually feel they have to respond helpfully. In reality, while some of these inquiries merit serious legal attention, others assuredly do not. The hope of most GCs is that they can organize themselves to become more selective; that they can move from being excessively reactive to being proactive. In other words, their job should be to anticipate problems before they arise. The focus should be on avoiding disputes rather than resolving them.

Legal risk can be managed in many ways, but the emphasis is usually on preventing non-lawyers in businesses from inadvertently exposing their organizations to some kind of liability (such as might flow from a breach of some regulation or of an agreement). This control of risk can be achieved, for example, by increasing legal awareness, by introducing protocols or procedures, by using standard documents, or by involving lawyers more directly in the affairs of organizations. Legal risk management can also involve the conduct of audits, risk reviews, and health checks to assess, for instance, an organization's processes for managing regulatory compliance or its preparedness for litigation. There is little question that tomorrow's in-house lawyers will become increasingly systematic and rigorous in their management of risk and will require sophisticated tools and techniques to help them. Strikingly, very few law firms have yet recognized the commercial opportunities here.

Another risk-related trend will be towards the greater sharing of risk between in-house lawyers and law firms. If deals and disputes do not conclude satisfactorily, some GCs believe that the law firms involved should suffer some of the downside, by reducing their fees. With some justification, law firms retort that this should cut both ways, so that the successful conclusion of a legal project should surely then result in an uplift in fees. No doubt, these debates on fees and risk-sharing will intensify in years to come, as economic pressures increase. New ways of allocating risks will evolve, in attempts to incentivize law firms in different ways. One arresting example of this is when in-house lawyers pay law firms bonuses if they help them to avoid litigation.

Knowledge Management

The use of standard documents, as said, is a well-established technique for reducing legal risk: non-lawyers and lawyers alike are required to use (and only then with permission) fixed-form agreements that have been carefully crafted in anticipation of well-known legal problems and pitfalls. Business people can be constrained in their negotiations by imposing the use of agreements with terms and conditions that cannot be altered without sign-off from lawyers.

The actual preparation of these standard documents belongs to the world of legal knowledge management. This is the process of capturing, nurturing, and sharing the collective know-how and expertise of a group of lawyers. The motive here is to avoid duplication of effort and to build an institutional memory that is superior to the recall of any individuals, no matter how talented. Knowledge management is one of the central jobs of professional support lawyers, a key group of legal specialists who work in major law firms, especially in the UK.

Significantly, in-house legal departments rarely employ knowledge managers and professional support lawyers. There is a paradox and inconsistency here. It would clearly be in the interests of in-house lawyers to secure the efficiencies that knowledge management would bring. In contrast, for law firms that charge by the hour, the incentive to become more efficient through knowledge recycling is less than immediately obvious. Why, then, do in-house lawyers generally hold back from recruiting knowledge managers whereas major law firms have invested heavily? For in-house lawyers, the deterrent seems to be the expense of employing professional support lawyers—it is difficult, I am told, to make the business case to chief finance officers for employing lawyers who do not advise directly on disputes or deals. As for law firms, they know that their clients (in the UK if less so in the US and Canada) expect their external advisers to have substantial bodies of templates and precedents; and knowledge managers are the people who specialize in maintaining this kind of know-how. In summary, most in-house lawyers like the idea of knowledge management but would prefer law firms to pay for it.

This will change. Before long, in-house lawyers will recognize and be able to quantify the benefits that professional support lawyers can bring and will manage to convince their boards that it makes sense to invest in people who will bring savings through IT-enabled legal knowledge sharing (within legal departments and between organizations too).

Expecting More From Law Firms

Moving away from risk and knowledge management, how will clients select law firms in the future? It is often assumed that what differentiates one lawyer or law firm from another is their sub-stantive expertise; that clients will gravitate towards lawyers who seem to know more or appear more deeply expert. However, cli-ents often say that there is little to choose between many good lawyers and good law firms, that they are equally and impres-sively familiar with black-letter law and market practice. What frequently distinguishes law firms, particularly when the work is genuinely bespoke, are the personal relationships that lawyers have with those they advise. (When the work is routine, the inter-personal dimension is of less importance.)

To run a successful legal business in the future, therefore, it will not be sufficient for lawyers to be in possession of fine legal minds. Tomorrow's lawyers will need to acquire various softer skills if they are to win new clients and keep them happy. In-house lawyers of the future will not only be more demanding on costs; they will be more discerning about the relationships they choose to cultivate with external firms. This will place pressures on law firms to make the most of face-to-face interactions and use social networking systems to maintain regular contact.

Already clients respond favourably, for example, to law firms which express ongoing, and even passionate, interest in them. They like to feel that the firms to which they pay substantial fees are bearing them in mind and have their interests at heart, even when not working together on a particular job. They appreci-ate those law firms which have clearly devoted their own time to thinking specifically about them and their business and their industry. Clients like to hear, for instance, about a deal that has been done that may be relevant to them. They appreciate periodic briefings on the trends and developments that may have a direct impact on them. Maintaining this sort of rolling contact does not come naturally to many lawyers and is often trumped by pieces of chargeable work for other clients. This is regrettable because this kind of regular interaction is increasingly vital for the long-term relationships that clients are now deeming important.

A related issue to which young lawyers should be sensitive is the need for law firms to empathize with their clients. GCs often observe that their external law firms do not understand their clients, that they have little insight into the daily dynamics and operations of their clients' businesses. It is not that the law firms fail, for instance, to read their clients' annual reports (although some do fall at this hurdle) or that they are ignorant of fundamentals of the sector in which their clients trade. Instead there is a wider worry: that law firms do not take sufficient time to immerse themselves in their clients' environments and get a feel for what it is actually like to work in their businesses. For example, it has been suggested to me that most firms do not grasp, in any given client, the tolerance and appetite for risk, the amount of administration and bureaucracy, the significance and extent and tone of internal communication, and, vitally, the broader strategic and business context of the deals and disputes upon which they advise.

In short, tomorrow's lawyers will need to be more in tune with tomorrow's clients. In contrast, when meeting with their clients today, many partners of law firms are said to broadcast and pontificate instead of listening to what is actually on the minds of those they are serving. In other words, many law firms lack empathy. They fail to put themselves in their clients' shoes and see the business from the clients' perspective. It is often claimed that, because they do not pause to listen, firms cannot distinguish between those occasions when a client wants quick, rough-and-ready guidance as opposed to detailed and exhaustive legal analysis. This lack of empathy and the inability to listen could be deeply prejudicial to long-term relationships between firms and clients in the future.

The More-For-Less Challenge

Although legal risk management and knowledge management will be key strategic issues for tomorrow's in-house lawyers and the quality and tone of their relationships with firms will be an important operational concern, the dominant management preoccupation of most GCs today is meeting the more-for-less challenge. In 2012, and for the foreseeable future, this is what is keeping most GCs awake at night. How can they deliver more legal service to their businesses at less cost?

The low-hanging fruit here is the possibility of driving down the fees of external lawyers. But there is a primal and fundamental tension: clients and lawyers have very different objectives. When a client phones a law firm and intimates that their business has a problem, it is an unusually virtuous partner who will not hope, deep down, that it is a big problem. For any piece of legal work, the client will invariably pray that their legal requirements are routine and can be disposed of quickly and painlessly, while a law firm will generally hanker after more challenging instructions that might occupy a team with complex work for quite some time.

There are other related tensions arising from the still-dominant practice of hourly billing. Most clients do not want to buy the time of experts. They want results, solutions, and practical commercial guidance. They also want certainty and predictability of costs, and not the open-ended commitment of the blank cheque that hourly billing often entails. Generally, hourly billing does not incentivize law firms to give clients what they actually want. Consequently, we will see, in the coming decade, as noted in relation to risk management, more sophisticated mechanisms for aligning the incentives of law firms and their clients.

These mechanisms will not be crude and ineffectual alternatives to hourly billing. In Chapter 2, I explain why these generally disappoint. Instead, in-house lawyers will come to the view, as discussed in that chapter, that the cost savings they need cannot be secured simply by pricing differently. Rather, the challenge is to work differently. Some in-house counsel have already arrived at this conclusion and so are wrestling, if but tentatively, with various alternative ways of sourcing legal services.

The underpinning thinking here bears repetition. Historically, legal work has been undertaken either by clients themselves or by their outside law firms. The problem with this is that it is proving too costly for routine and repetitive legal tasks to be discharged within firms and legal departments. And so, different approaches to sourcing such work are now gaining some traction: outsourcing to third party providers in low-cost countries; off-shoring legal work to locations where businesses have already transferred other functions, such as call centres; encouraging law firms to subcontract to practices in less costly regions; or using contract lawyers who charge about half the price of traditional law firms. These are all instances of what I call, in Chapter 2, the 'efficiency strategy'—cutting the costs of legal service.

Yet another possibility is co-sourcing, which can involve a group of in-house departments coming together and sharing the cost of some common legal service, perhaps by setting up shared services centres. This is an example of the 'collaboration strategy' outlined in Chapter 2, where I mention the ways in which banks and local authorities are already cooperating.

There is no doubt that the in-house community is becoming steadily more interested in these and many other new ways of sourcing legal work.

The Collaborative Spirit

A different form of cooperation is also emerging—some in-house lawyers are keen to engender a collaborative spirit amongst their external law firms. They speak of their primary law firms as their 'extended family'. The intention here is that firms trust rather than compete with one another; and that their collective energies are directed at supporting the client instead of jockeying for position for the next tranche of work. The result should be a more productive, efficient, and civilized group of lawyers. On this view, the legal capability of an organization is the combination of the in-house function and its external firms. The lawyers from the firms are expected to work together as a family—not one that is dysfunctional and constantly bickering but one that shares and focuses relentlessly on a larger common purpose: the interests of clients.

This approach to managing external law firms is not yet common. Indeed some GCs are sceptical about inter-firm cooperation. Many banks seem to fall into this camp. They maintain that it is plainly unrealistic to expect their principal external firms to collaborate. Hard-nosed lawyers want a market and not a social club or a family outing. Some in-house lawyers therefore actively encourage their firms to compete strenuously with one another. On this more combative approach, firms are frequently invited to bid against one another, and to demonstrate their supremacy—that they are better, less costly, more efficient, or more innovative than the rest.

Although there are no right answers here, I have seen both schools in action (within and beyond the financial services sector) and predict that the collaboration camp will win out. This approach holds obvious attractions: duplication of effort can be avoided; asymmetries can be eliminated; energies are more efficiently channelled towards the clients; and working relationships are more amicable. It simply makes sense, for example, from the clients' point of view, for their external firms to coordinate in the provision of training services. Exciting opportunities also emerge such as being able to assemble 'dream teams', made up of the best lawyers, hand-selected from across various firms, and purpose-built for particular deals and disputes. The challenge for those who favour family over feud is to put the incentives in the right place, so that law firms genuinely want to cooperate rather than compete. Half the battle here is for the client to ensure a more or less steady flow of work for firms who are family members. It will make sense on this collaborative approach for participants to embrace social networking technologies. These will bring firms under the one virtual roof and encourage and enable them to work in virtual groups. This could be done using generic services such as LinkedIn or legal tools such as Legal OnRamp. As in so many other areas of legal practice, the future for in-house lawyers will be digital.

Strategy for GCs

In practical terms, how are GCs preparing for the future and, in particular, addressing the more-for-less challenge? I cannot answer that question across the board but I have found that four broad strategies are in play, each differing in its scope and ambition. The first strategy has been for GCs to concentrate largely on external law firms and to drive their prices down. This is the preferred method of GCs who pass much of their legal work to external law firms. The second approach, better suited to large in-house departments, has been to focus instead on reshaping the in-house departments. The third has been simultaneously to review internal and external capabilities and seek to streamline both. The fourth tack has been the most ambitious—to start with a blank sheet of paper, to forget the current resources (in-house and outside) and instead to undertake a comprehensive legal needs analysis for the business. Once this analysis has been completed, the task then has been to identify dispassionately how best to resource the full set of needs; drawing not just on conventional lawyers but on the new legal providers too. This final strategy, in my view, is the one that will deliver the most cost-effective and responsive legal services for large businesses in the future and, in due course, will be the preferred approach of all competent in-house functions.

The Power and Responsibility of In-House Lawyers

I often find, somewhat surprisingly, that in-house lawyers betray a lack of self-confidence when contemplating the future.

Frequently they ask me if I expect law firms to revert to their old ways of working when the economy picks up. I invariably respond that it is almost entirely up to them, as the customers, to shape the answer to that query. If in-house lawyers do not want reinstatement of bad past habits, they must send that message very clearly to their external advisers. They can be assured that, in the current buyers' market, such a message cannot be ignored.

Most in-house lawyers will concede, in principle, that change is necessary and that they should run a tighter ship and drive a harder bargain with their suppliers, but most also claim that they do not seem to have the time, energy, or competence to introduce efficiency or collaboration solutions. When I probe more deeply, it transpires that many GCs would prefer off-the-shelf answers developed by law firms. However, and this is something of a vicious circle, there is, as noted, little incentive for law firms themselves to support either the efficiency or the collaboration strategy. Why should law firms destabilize their current businesses with potentially disruptive innovations when clients often seem indifferent and competitors themselves are inactive?

In-house lawyers must also remember that they are likely themselves to come under the microscope within their own organizations. It will not be plausible for them simply to complain ad infinitum about law firms' unwillingness to change. As it becomes widely known, for instance, that it is possible to source legal work in different ways, chief executives, chief finance officers, and boards will inevitably ask their GCs whether their departments are adapting and exploiting the opportunities afforded by these new ways of working. To help focus in-house lawyers' minds, I express this likely demand in terms of what I call the 'shareholder test':

> when a costed proposal for the conduct of a deal or dispute is being considered, would a commercially astute shareholder, who was familiar with the growing number of alternative ways of sourcing legal work, consider what is contemplated as representing value for money?

If in-house lawyers allow law firms to return to pre-recession billing and working practices, they will plainly fail the shareholder test. Soon in-house lawyers will have little choice but to overhaul their departments and working practices: the more-for-less pressure will build to an almost intolerable level and they will have to re-calibrate if not re-engineer the way they work internally and how they source external legal services.

In-house lawyers will flourish only if they can add relevant value that cannot be delivered by competing sources of legal service. The genuinely expert and trusted in-house legal adviser, who lives and breathes the business, should always be an invaluable resource, but unless GCs are also prepared to drive the efficiency and collaboration strategies within their own departments and across law firms as well as other providers that serve them, then their future is far from clear. I advise in-house lawyers not to wait until their platform is burning. Now is the time to prepare for the challenge.

They should remember (although many do not seem fully to grasp this) that they have immense purchasing power. Today and for many years to come, for major clients especially, it is likely to be a buyers' market. I struggle to understand why GCs have not driven external law firms much harder. The world's leading 100 law firms are sustained very largely by the world's top 1,000 businesses. If and when GCs become radically more demanding, they will have it within their power to urge a reshaping of this top echelon of firms and, in turn, redefine the entire legal marketplace.

8 | The Timing of the Changes

I am often asked to indicate the likely time scales of the changes that I predict. Some commentators and lawyers believe these changes are already upon us and that the legal world will have transformed within a very few years. Others maintain that the shifts will progress at a more plodding rate and that it will be some decades before the revolution is complete. I believe that we will witness neither a big bang revolution nor a slow burn evolution. Instead I expect an incremental revolution to unfold, in three stages—denial, re-sourcing, and disruption (see Figure 8.1).

I am not suggesting that all law firms and in-house legal departments will move evenly through these three stages in concert. Some pioneers will progress far more rapidly, while there will be laggards aplenty who will take much longer to advance. Like all models, this one is a simplification. Its purpose is to give a broad sense of the order in which most large law firms and in-house legal departments will move forward. The speed with which they move cannot be predicted with precision: this will depend largely on factors such as the state of the economy, the intensity of the demands made by clients, the impact of new competitors on the market, and whether or not a few firms take a positive lead in changing the way that legal services are delivered.

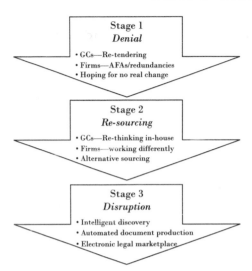

FIGURE 8.1 The three stages of change

Stage 1—Denial

During the first stage (and, as I write, in May 2012, we are still at this stage), the great majority of lawyers, both in firms and in-house, are wishing it were 2006 again. At that time, many law firms had more work than they could handle, with the added benefit that it was not price sensitive. As for in-house legal departments, although there were hints then that they would need to think about tightening their belts, they were generally not under pressure within their organizations to spend less. This was a time of plenty. It was a sellers' market and the buyers' purses were brimming.

In 2007, with the economic downturn and then crisis, came the start of the more-for-less challenge, as introduced in Chapter

1. The response of many General Counsel has been to seek to reduce their legal expenses, not by fundamentally changing their own internal operations and sourcing strategies, but by asking their external law firms for a significant reduction in fees. This has been done fairly formally in many cases through competitive tendering processes. In turn, most law firms have proposed a variety of alternative fee arrangements (AFAs) while also making many lawyers (from junior lawyers through to partners) and support staff redundant, and spending less on back-office functions such as technology and marketing.

In truth, most in-house legal departments and law firms are eager to weather the storm without major upheaval: in-house lawyers hope to maintain their headcount, while law firms strive, through (non-fundamental) cuts, to maintain their profitability. And this spirit lives on in 2012.

During this first stage, some law firms have been engaging in tokenism of a kind—they have been partaking of some modest alternative sourcing, but largely as a matter of show. Their purpose has been to construct a credible narrative to relay to those clients who inquire as to their cost-cutting strategies. The deeper purpose is to play for time. This is a stalling strategy, adopted in the hope that the market will return and clients will no longer have an urgent need to spend less on law firms.

At the same time, some in-house lawyers have argued that the answer for them has been to increase the size of their in-house department, on the ground that in-house lawyers cost less than legal specialists in law firms. This will often prove to be tactically flawed. It is an approach that can make unrealistic assumptions about how fully occupied the in-house lawyers will be. Also, supply often increases demand so that recruiting one in-house lawyer often leads to that person asking for an assistant and then a team. And, in any event, growing the in-house capability is often to fall back on the outmoded view that there are only two ways of sourcing legal work—within a department or through a law firm—and so ignores the possibility of alternative sourcing.

In summary, in this first stage, and it will run for a couple of years yet, I suggest most (but by no means all) lawyers are in denial of the fundamental and structural changes within the legal marketplace. They are assuming, or praying, that when the economic tide turns and business improves, then the legal world will return to its modus operandi of around 2006. This seems to me entirely implausible, partly because global economic conditions are unlikely to improve in the foreseeable future and in part because those who are running client businesses have now seen that legal costs can be managed more tightly, that legal work can be undertaken differently and more efficiently, and so they have no appetite for a return to the old inefficiencies.

Stage 2—Re-Sourcing

In due course, chief executives and boards will notice that legal costs are not plummeting as directed. General Counsel will have spoken optimistically to chief finance officers about reductions in hourly rates and alternative fee arrangements, but it will become clear that the promised reductions are not materializing. Lawyers, both in-house and in firms, will need to move from pricing differently to working differently.

It will not suffice, in this second stage, for General Counsel to ignore the inefficiencies in their own departments. Just as they will have asked law firms to find alternative ways of sourcing the routine work that used to be done at high hourly rates by junior lawyers, so too they will need to apply this same approach within their own legal businesses. Together, therefore, law firms and in-house legal departments will analyse their legal work and identify ways that the most straightforward, procedural, and administrative-based activities and tasks can be sourced differently, whether by outsourcing, off-shoring, using paralegals, computerizing, or deploying any of the various sourcing strategies laid out in Chapter 4. In-house departments will also begin to collaborate more with one another, sharing the costs of legal services in the manner anticipated in the collaboration strategy (Chapter 2).

At this stage, the new third party providers of services to the legal profession—legal process outsourcers, publishers, accounting firms, private equity-backed start-ups, and many more—will also come to play a more pivotal role in the delivery of legal services. There may not be a tipping point, but we are likely to witness a significant upsurge in new competition for law firms.

Additionally, in this second stage, law firms and in-house departments will find ways of running their own back offices (technology and accounts, for example) at far lower costs. This could be through business process outsourcing or shared services facilities.

And there is also likely to be a shift in this second stage towards greater investment by in-house legal departments in legal needs analysis and legal risk management. Owners and leaders of businesses will want to have a far clearer sense of what are the urgent and unavoidable legal expenses and may confine their legal spend to these alone.

Stage 3—Disruption

In Stage 2, alternative sourcing will usually be achieved by requiring legal work to be undertaken by lower-cost labour. Effectively, this will be a form of labour arbitrage, and it will result in great savings. However, it will not be the end-game in the development of the legal marketplace. Much more radical transformation will come about in Stage 3, through the introduction of ever more powerful information technologies. In the main, these technologies will be disruptive, that is, they will challenge and displace the traditional way in which legal work has been done in the past.

Many lawyers and commentators fail to recognize that services such as legal process outsourcing (LPO) are likely to be temporary measures and not long-term solutions. If we think of two classes of service that are typically considered to be suitable for LPO—document review in litigation and basic contract drafting—both of these will in due course be replaced by information systems that can outperform junior lawyers and administrative staff. The very features of these areas of legal work that make them suitable for LPO—that they can be broken down into manageable parts, and that they can be discharged by well-trained but relatively unskilled human beings with the assistance of detailed procedures—are also precisely the features of work that make them amenable to the application of IT. Thus, advanced search technologies used for electronic disclosure are already outperforming human beings who conduct document review in litigation. (Electronic disclosure, or e-disclosure, broadly speaking, involves parties to a dispute letting one another know about the existence of relevant, electronically stored documents.) And, likewise, automated document assembly systems can already operate more reliably and efficiently than modestly experienced lawyers and administrators.

The widespread and pervasive deployment of disruptive technologies represents the end-game for legal service although, even then, as noted in Chapter 1, there is no finishing line in the world of IT. In the long run, increasing amounts of legal work can and will be taken on by advanced computer systems, with a light hand on the tiller from the human beings who are their users. This will be the context and backdrop of the careers and working lives of tomorrow's lawyers.

These disruptive technologies will come to dominate not just in substantive legal work but also in the way in which providers of legal services (both human beings and computer systems) are selected. Price comparison systems, reputation systems, and online auctions for legal services (see Chapter 5) will be used frequently, creating an electronic legal marketplace quite unlike the traditional basis of legal trading that has endured for decades and more.

It is not that computer systems will replace all legal work by, say, 2020. Of course not. But around that time and from then on it will become commonplace across the legal profession for all substantial and successful legal businesses to be converting their business processes from human handcrafting to ever more sophisticated and intelligent IT-based production. We have seen such changes in many other sectors of our economy and there is no reason to think that the law should be immune from IT. If analogous technologies can transform the practice of medicine and audit, then lawyers should be open to similar overhaul.

A legal world will emerge that is manifestly different from today's. And it is into this world that most young lawyers will be stepping. For those aspiring lawyers who hoped for a career akin to that enjoyed by lawyers of their parents' generation, they will be disappointed. For those who seek new opportunities and wish to participate in bringing about the advances that I predict in this book, I believe there has never been a more exciting time.

9 | Access to Justice and Online Legal Services

In 2000, in my book *Transforming the Law*, I predicted that, within five years, more people in the UK would have access to the Internet than access to justice. Unfortunately, I have been proven correct. Today, as I explain shortly, only 5 per cent of British people are effectively excluded from the Internet, whereas the majority of citizens in England and Wales are unable to afford most of the services of lawyers and of the courts. The good news, as I have for long claimed, is that information technology will be pivotal in overcoming many of the growing problems of access to justice. My aim in this chapter is to show how this might come to pass.

Access to Justice

Franz Kafka sets the scene hauntingly in *The Trial*. He tells of a gatekeeper who inexplicably refuses to grant a man access to the law. This unfortunate man from the country had not expected any problems. After all, he thinks, 'the law should be accessible to everyone at all times'. So it might be thought, but research in England and Wales conducted a few years ago concluded that around one million civil justice problems go unresolved each year. This legal exclusion or unmet legal need is a grave social problem and is loosely referred to as the 'access to justice' problem.

Thinking more widely for a moment, no one today can pretend to have mastery over anything other than small parts of our legal system. And yet every one of us, under the law, is taken to have knowledge of all legal provisions that affect us. Given that most citizens do not know most of the law and cannot afford to obtain conventional legal advice, we seem to be in a rather parlous state. The problem perhaps comes most sharply into focus when people contemplate taking an action through the court system. From a lay perspective, as well as appearing to be unaffordable, the courts seem to be excessively time-consuming, unjustifiably combative, and inexplicably steeped in opaque procedure and language. It was with such problems in mind that, in 1995 and 1996, Lord Woolf, then a Law Lord and later the Lord Chief Justice of England and Wales, published *Access to Justice*, his two seminal reports on the future of the civil justice system.

Lord Woolf's terms of reference confined his attention to the resolution of disputes. And for many judges and policymakers since, the idea of improving access to justice has come to mean improving the way disputes are resolved. I take a wider view. To be entirely or even substantially focused on dispute resolution in our pursuit of justice is, I claim, to miss much that we should expect of our legal systems. It is my contention that better access to justice should embrace improvements not just to dispute resolution but also to what I call dispute containment, dispute avoidance, and legal health promotion.

Dispute containment concentrates on preventing disagreements that have arisen from escalating excessively; and it is lawyers as well as the parties themselves who need to be contained.

Dispute avoidance is a theme that in-house lawyers often raise with me: they speak of legal risk management, or as I put it, putting a fence at the top of a cliff rather than an ambulance at the bottom. I have yet to meet a regular human being, whether a chief executive or a consumer, who would prefer a large dispute neatly resolved by lawyers to not having one in the first place.

Legal health promotion extends beyond the preventative lawyering of dispute avoidance to ensuring that people are aware of and able to take advantage of the many benefits, improvements, and advantages that the law can confer, even if no problem has arisen.

Recognition, Selection, and Service

With these four dimensions of access to justice in mind, the plot thickens somewhat when we reflect on the plight of the non-lawyer. The first obstacle for the non-lawyer is recognition, the process by which someone with no legal insight realizes that they would benefit from legal help. Sometimes it is obvious— when a claim arrives through the letterbox or a decision has been made to move house. But often non-lawyers may not know that they are in a situation in which there is a legal problem to be resolved, contained, avoided, or that there is some benefit to be secured. Paradoxically, it seems you need to be a lawyer to know if and when you would benefit from legal help.

The second challenge, even if our non-lawyer has recognized that he or she would benefit from legal help, is to select the best source of legal guidance, whether that be finding a suitable lawyer or some other kind of adviser or even online help.

The third dimension is the delivery of legal service itself. And here we find the wide range of options that people now face in what I call a multi-sourcing environment (see Chapter 4). In relation to this third challenge, I do not believe that conventional lawyers in traditional law firms are always the best placed or most affordable sources of guidance for clients. It seems almost inevitable that cuts in legal aid brought about by economic conditions will lead to legal and court services that are less affordable and less accessible. A major and urgent social challenge is to find new ways of providing legal help, not least to citizens and to small businesses.

Online Legal Services

One clear alternative to the provision of legal help by lawyers is for skilled and often voluntary non-lawyers to advise people on their problems, rights, and responsibilities. In the UK, for instance, the Citizens Advice service does precisely this but it too suffers from lack of resources. Another option is to provide citizens and businesses with online legal resources so that they can take care of some of their legal affairs on their own; or, when guidance is needed, they can work more efficiently with their legal advisers. If we can have in England, for example, NHS Direct, an online service that provides medical guidance, then why not have something similar for law?

Online services generally are no longer just for a high-tech minority. On the contrary, the Internet is now central to the lives of the majority of families and businesses in England and Wales. In a recent study, *The Internet in Britain, 2011*, the Oxford Internet Institute established that 73 per cent of the British population are now users and that 57 per cent of British Internet users have used at least one online government service in the past year. The remaining 27 per cent are, of course, important; but only about one-fifth of these non-users (or ex-users) 'definitely don't know' someone who could assist them. This means that around 5 per cent are currently out of reach. This is a smaller percentage than is often supposed.

As for online legal facilities, these can come in three forms: first, as free Web-based services, provided by a variety of commercial and not-for-profit organizations; second, as subscription-based tools from conventional law firms; and, third, as chargeable offerings from other businesses, such as alternative business structures or legal publishers.

In practice, then, how might the Internet actually help to secure access to justice in all the various aspects I note? In the first instance, addressing the initial obstacle noted above, IT can and will continue to be of use in assisting non-lawyers to *recognize* that they might benefit from some kind of legal input. One approach will be for people to register their social and working interests and for legal alerts to be delivered automatically to them when there are new laws or changes in old law that apply to them. Another tack will be online triage—when a citizen has a grievance of some sort, a simple online diagnostic system could ask a series of questions, require some boxes to be ticked, and could then identify if the user has a legal issue, and if so, of what sort.

A further possibility, as mentioned in Chapter 5, will be the embedding of legal rules into systems and procedures. Consider the game of Solitaire. When I was a boy, we played this with atoms (playing cards). It was possible, when using these cards, to place a red 4 beneath a red 5, although this would clearly have been in breach of the rules. But it would have been physically possible. In contrast, when you play Solitaire on your computer, such a move is not possible. Any attempt to place a red 4 below a red 5 will be met with a refusal by the system to do as clicked. The difference here is that, with the electronic version, the rules are embedded in the system. Failure to comply is not an option. In years to come, in many dimensions of our social and working lives, I predict that legal rules will similarly be embedded in our systems and processes. This means that non-lawyers will no longer have to worry about, or have the responsibility of, recognizing when legal input is required.

A final use of IT to help non-lawyers recognize when they need legal help will be through what I call 'communities of legal experience'. If you are a PC user and have been confronted with some incomprehensible error message from Windows, you will no doubt have cut and pasted the message into Google, and found that someone out there has already provided an explanation and solution to your problem. So too in law, I believe that, in open source and wiki spirit, large communities of legal experience will build up so that people will learn of legal issues that affect them, not formally through notification by their lawyers but informally through their social networks.

IT will also play a role in helping clients *select* their lawyers and other sources of guidance. As explained in Chapter 5, there will be online reputation systems, not unlike those services that offer collective feedback on hotels and restaurants, which will provide insight from other clients into their experiences with particular law firms and lawyers. There will also be price comparison systems, which will allow non-lawyers to assess the respective prices of competing legal providers. And there will be auctions for legal services—not generally for complex bespoke work but for the routine and repetitive work that I say will be sourced in various ways in the future.

As for the role of IT in the delivery of legal *service*, increasingly people will turn for basic guidance, on procedural and substantive issues, not to lawyers but to online legal services. We already use so much online information in our daily lives that there is no reason, especially for those who cannot afford otherwise, why legal help should not be similarly accessed. Equally, users will turn to the Internet for the production of standard documents, such as basic wills and landlord and tenant agreements (see Chapter 3), and to communities of legal experience to determine how fellow lay people have sorted out their difficulties in the past.

Another possibility, as described in Chapter 10, is online dispute resolution (ODR), which are Internet-based methods—for example, e-mediation and e-negotiation—for resolving people's differences.

Yet another prospect will be to build social networks of lawyers or legal advisers who are willing, in their own time rather than on a face-to-face basis, to provide guidance, in a variety of ways, across the Internet (either directly to citizens or indirectly to advice workers).

Although I speak of many of these systems as belonging to the future, there are already innumerable examples of operational online legal services. In the words of William Gibson, the science fiction writer, 'The future has already arrived. It's just not evenly distributed yet.' It is early days to be sure, but within a small number of years these systems will be commonplace in helping non-lawyers to recognize when they need legal help and to select the best sources of advice, as well as in actually offering them practical guidance. And this is not just the pipe dream of some Internet enthusiasts. Significantly, recent research by the Legal Services Board in England and Wales found that there is considerable enthusiasm amongst consumers for the online delivery of reliable legal support and advice.

Some of these uses of online legal services will be 'disruptive' for traditional law firms, in the sense discussed in Chapter 5. But, at the same time, many of these techniques will make the law available to people who would otherwise have no affordable sources of legal help. This I call the realization of the 'latent legal market'—those countless occasions in the lives of many people when they need legal help and would benefit from legal help but, until now, they have been unable to secure this assistance (whether to resolve, contain, or avoid problems, or indeed to afford them some benefit). Online legal service, therefore, will liberate the latent legal market.

10 | Judges, IT, Virtual Courts, and ODR

In 1981, while still an undergraduate in law at the University of Glasgow, I wrote an undergraduate dissertation on computers and the judicial process. My interest was in the extent to which the work of judges could be supported or even replaced by advanced computer systems. The potential and limitations of judicial technology continue to fascinate me and I have had the good fortune to be able to explore my thinking further in collaboration with a number of England's most senior judges, especially in my capacity as IT Adviser to the Lord Chief Justice, a position I have held since 1998.

Judges and IT

Judges are commonly portrayed, by the media and in fiction, as old-fashioned and otherworldly. Consistent with this view, you might expect the judiciary in advanced jurisdictions to be made up of the last of the neo-Luddites. The reverse is so. Most judges with whom I work and speak are now committed users of IT and are keen to embrace systems that offer practical benefits in their everyday work, such as email, word processing, and online research.

Looking beyond these rudimentary applications, how profoundly could IT affect the work of judges? In the early 1980s, I came to the conclusion that it was neither possible (technically) nor desirable (in principle) for computers fully to take over the work of judges. My position on this has not changed. Judicial decision-making in hard cases, especially when judges are called upon to handle complex issues of principle, policy, and morality, is well beyond the capabilities of current and foreseeable computer systems.

However, I believe that some of the techniques and lessons of this book can be applied to judges as much as to other lawyers. Consistent with the ideas of decomposing and multi-sourcing as introduced in Chapter 4, I can see no compelling argument, for example, against analysing and dividing judicial work into separate parts and, where appropriate, finding alternative and more efficient ways of undertaking some of these tasks.

Judges frequently tell me that they are called upon to undertake mountains of administration that others, less qualified, could handle on their behalf. At the same time, there is scope for standardization of at least parts of the documents (the directions and orders, for instance) that judges create. More, the judiciary would clearly benefit from the use of document assembly technology, where much of what appears in these final documents is standard wording with minor variations (see Chapter 3).

Initial legal research could also be conducted in different ways, as is already demonstrated to a limited extent by the deployment of judicial assistants in the Court of Appeal and in the Supreme Court. While it would not be feasible to use these junior lawyers across the entire system, there are other innovative ways (using IT) that know-how and experience could be shared. I am calling, therefore, at the very least, for serious, further investigation of the scope for the decomposing and multi-sourcing of judicial work. So far, senior judges have met this call open-mindedly and so I expect change in the direction noted.

As for information technology, most conceivable systems for judges are 'sustaining' in the language of Chapter 1. However, there is one category of system—online dispute resolution (ODR)— that could conceivably challenge the conventional judicial role. I turn to this later in the chapter.

Disappointing Progress

One area in which there is judicial disappointment in most juris-dictions is in applications that fall under the broad heading of 'e-working'. The grievance here is that the systems that are avail-able to judges do not generally support them directly in the every-day management of their cases and documents.

The term 'e-working' is deployed in different senses in the judicial world. Sometimes it is used synonymously with the 'electronic case file', the idea of which is that all documents relat-ing to particular cases are submitted (e-filed) to the courts in electronic form and are available to the judges and officials as electronic bundles. On other occasions, 'e-working' is used in a broader sense to include the electronic case file and one or both of workflow and project management (see Chapter 5). Whatever terminology is preferred, this broader definition nicely captures the vision that court technologists around the world share:

IT-based workflow or project management to streamline and enhance standard process and electronic case files for better management of the documents themselves.

In England and Wales, it is undeniable that little technological progress has been made over the last 20 years either towards e-working or in the administration and management of the courts. The organization of much of the work of the courts remains labour-intensive, cumbersome, and paper-based. A visit to most courts in England and Wales reveals a working environment that is less efficient and automated than most ordinary offices in the country, whether in the public or private sector. Across the country, judges complain of antiquated systems, outdated working practices, excessive running costs, inefficiencies, errors, and delays. In turn, court users suffer and the reputation of the justice system is adversely affected. In his *Access to Justice* reports, Lord Woolf made a series of recommendations in the mid-1990s for the computerization of much of the civil justice system. Very few have been implemented.

The lack of progress can be attributed to two main factors: insufficient investment by the Government and the Treasury, which have not considered civil justice to be a priority; and the Ministry of Justice's poor track record of successfully procuring and delivering large-scale technology projects.

Incidentally, there has been no shortage of vision from within the justice system. Over the years, a number of enlightened judges, politicians, and civil servants have expressed bold views of a court and justice system transformed through technology. There has been sufficient vision but insufficient cash and IT capability.

Yet, the lack of progress so far should not deter us from looking ahead and anticipating change that is likely for tomorrow's lawyers if not for today's.

The Way Ahead

If courts and tribunals were easily affordable, widely accessible, and delivered a swift service, an argument could be made for ignoring the new and emerging technologies. But today's court system is creaking. Too often, it is inefficient, slow, and too costly. As noted in the previous chapter, around one million civil justice problems are said to go unresolved every year and the projected cuts in legal aid will greatly add to this shocking level of legal exclusion. Access to justice is in grave danger of being available only to the rich. More than this, full-scale civil litigation at disproportionate expense is, too often, wielding a sledgehammer to miss a nut.

In principle, if the advantages of IT that are seen in other sectors were enjoyed by the courts, the labour-intensive, cumbersome, and paper-based systems for court administration could be replaced by an automated, streamlined, and largely paper-free set of systems that would be less costly, less prone to error, more efficient, and more accessible. In turn, an efficient and well-equipped court system, populated by satisfied lawyers, would be a system in which the public would have greater confidence. There is an international dimension too. If England seriously aspires to being a leading global centre of excellence for the resolution of disputes, then there should be state-of-the-art, leading-edge systems, processes, and infrastructure in place to support this.

Ministers of the UK's Coalition Government, however, have not yet shown their hand on the question of IT in support of court administration. Looking forward, they (and politicians around the world) would be well advised to embrace IT in support of dispute resolution. Their preoccupation, understandably, may currently be with cutting costs rather than investing in technology. But the irony here, in this period of austerity, is that IT is a solution for governments and not a problem. The prize is a glittering one—inexpensive, swift, proportionate, inclusive resolution of disputes.

It would be naïve in the midst and aftermath of the recession to expect a huge injection of investment into outdated courts and court systems around the world. But policymakers could fruitfully articulate and promote a long-term vision that should help to direct what will inevitably be an incremental transformation of the courts.

IT-Enabled Courts

Looking beyond back-office administration and e-working, what is now technologically possible in the courts themselves? First of all, even before parties assemble in court, there is one technique that can be of immediate benefit—e-filing. This involves the submission of documents to the court in electronic form, which can be so much more convenient for judges and administrators than huge bundles of paper, especially if the e-filed pages are hyperlinked to one another.

Next, in the courtroom itself, one obvious use of IT is for the judge to take notes as cases progress on a laptop or desktop computer. Three further, more sophisticated, technologies have been used, to a greater or lesser extent, in courts around the world since the early 1990s. The first is computer-assisted transcription (CAT), which enables words spoken in the courtroom to be captured by stenographers and then converted into text that appears almost instantaneously on the screens of judges and other participants. The text can be annotated as it appears and a searchable database of the proceedings is created.

Second are document display systems, which ensure that everyone in a hearing is, literally, on the same page—instead of waiting for all parties and judges to locate papers and files manually, the court's attention can be directed to a particular page by asking all participants to look at their screens, which instantly display relevant documents.

Research and experience suggest that using CAT and document display technologies reduces the length of hearings by one-quarter to one-third.

The third technology is electronic presentation of evidence (EPE) and reflects the old adage that a picture is worth a thousand words. Rather than relying exclusively on oral advocacy, lawyers can present evidence using a wide range of non-verbal tools, including charts, graphs, diagrams, drawings, models, animations, reconstructions, and simulations. These can be displayed in the courtroom on individual monitors or projected onto very large screens. They can be used in both civil and criminal cases—for instance, the extent of a delay in a project can be demonstrated powerfully by an animation that compares actual with projected time taken, or complex movements of funds can be captured in a simple graphic rather than by convoluted oral summary.

As for actual use of CAT, document display systems, and electronic presentation of evidence, here too take-up has been extremely low across the court system, despite the time and cost savings. But there have been a few notable exceptions. The new UK Supreme Court supports e-filing, document display, real-time transcription, judicial use of computers on the bench, and remote evidence. And various tribunals have impressive systems. Each, however, is an oasis in an otherwise arid desert of technology-free hearing rooms.

These systems have enjoyed greatest success in public inquiries such as the high-tech Bloody Sunday Inquiry by Lord Saville (where the resources for setting up the hearing rooms have been less constrained), large-scale commercial disputes (where the parties themselves have substantial litigation budgets), and complex criminal cases (the criminal justice system has received much greater investment in its IT than the civil justice system).

In the future, many courtrooms will look like Lord Saville's Inquiry hearing rooms; not unlike NASA control centres.

Virtual Courts

Looking further ahead now, in thinking about the long-term future of courts and dispute resolution, one fundamental question sets the agenda: is court a service or a place? To resolve disputes, do parties and their advisers need to congregate together in one physical space, in order to present arguments to a judge? Why not have virtual courts or online dispute resolution?

The terminology is not firmly settled but, generally, when reference is made to 'virtual courts', this is to a fairly conventional courtroom set-up into which some video link is introduced. Take-up has been greatest in criminal cases, where there are child or intimidated witnesses; and, increasingly, for bail and remand hearings, conducted through links between prisons and courts. In some civil cases, witnesses from outside the UK have given evidence remotely, as have otherwise inaccessible expert witnesses. The idea is that the witnesses or the accused appear on large screens, suitably located in hearing rooms, and this saves time and money or protects the vulnerable.

In 2010, the Ministry of Justice in the UK published a report on this subject. It was entitled, 'Virtual Court Pilot: Outcome Evaluation'. On the face of it, the findings suggested that the costs of the enabling technologies outweigh the benefits secured. However, the costs of these systems are plummeting, especially if procured in bulk. Crucially, also, the report did establish that a video link between a police station and a court can be used successfully to conduct a first hearing in the majority of criminal cases—and, in the pilot, it reduced the average time from charge to first hearing, it cut down the failure-to-appear rates, and it saved the costs of transporting prisoners from prisons to courts.

The growing use across society of video-calling and video-conferencing—from Skype to 'telepresence' (which is like Skype on steroids)—suggests there is enormous scope for virtual courts, if not for trials then for earlier hearings, when judges could sit in their chambers and all participants could attend remotely.

For tomorrow's lawyers, appearance in physical courtrooms may become a rarity. Instead, virtual appearances will become the norm, and new presentational and advocacy skills will be required. I am not suggesting that virtual courtrooms will be pervasive in the short or medium term. Virtual hearings are very rarely held in England, other than, occasionally, to enable vulnerable witnesses to give evidence and for a very few remand hearings. But they will become commonplace in due course, I have little doubt.

Online Dispute Resolution

In the virtual courtroom set-up, one or more judges sit in some kind of hearing room, dispensing justice in the traditional manner. The break from tradition here is that some participants appear virtually across some video link rather than in person. But there is a step beyond the virtual hearing and this is known as online dispute resolution.

With ODR, no traditional courtroom is involved. Instead, the process of resolving a dispute, especially the formulation of the solution, is entirely or largely conducted through the Internet. A leading example of ODR is Cybersettle, a Web-based system that was launched in 1998. Cybersettle is claimed to have handled over 200,000 claims of combined value in excess of $1.6 billion. Most of the cases have been personal injury or insurance claims. It uses a process known as 'double-blind bidding'—a claimant and defendant each submit the highest and lowest settlement figures that would be acceptable to them. These amounts are not disclosed but if the two ranges overlap, a settlement can be achieved, the final figure usually being a split down the middle.

Another sort of ODR is mediation across the Web. An online mediation can be undertaken when a face-to-face mediation is logistically difficult, perhaps because of the locations of the parties or when, relative to the size of dispute, it is too costly to assemble. Mediation is one form of ADR (alternative dispute resolution), a way of sorting out differences beyond the courts. Instead, the mediator, as a third party, assists parties to negotiate settlements, usually on a private and confidential basis. Using a mix of Web-based tools and human mediators, through email exchanges and online discussion areas, conflicts can be resolved electronically by e-mediation. Parties to a dispute can, in this way, settle their disagreements across the Internet without convening in a meeting room.

A blend of ODR techniques is used to sort out problems on eBay. About 60 million disputes arise each year amongst eBay

users. It is unimaginable that these would all get resolved in conventional courts. Instead, ODR is used—swiftly, efficiently, and
generally to good effect.

The Ministry of Justice in England and Wales has also embraced
ODR. Its Money Claim Online system was launched in 2002 and
enables users, with no legal experience, to recover money owed
to them without needing to handle complex forms or set foot in
a county court. The service covers claims, such as unpaid debts,
up to a value of £100,000. It allows a claimant to request a claim
online, keep track of the status of the claim and, where appropriate, request entry of judgment and enforcement. Defendants
can also use the online system and it is said to handle more than
60,000 claims each year, which is a greater throughput than any
single county court in England and Wales.

Very few law firms have yet taken ODR seriously. In fact, even
though the European Commission has formulated a draft regulation on ODR, most lawyers have not even heard of online dispute
resolution. I predict that ODR will prove to be a disruptive technology that fundamentally challenges the work of traditional litigators
(and of judges). In the long run, I expect it to become the dominant
way to resolve all but the most complex and high-value disputes.
For law firms and court lawyers, this is a direct assault on their
conventional work. But it is also a great opportunity—to become a
leading player in this new, currently uncontested, market space.

Fair Trial?

Virtual courts and ODR may, however, be seen as threatening everyday conceptions of fair trials. For example, victims

of crimes and their families, alongside aggrieved and wronged parties in civil disputes, may feel short-changed by a lack of physical meeting. An IT-enabled resolution may not provide the closure that some regard as a central part of the judicial process. On the other hand, if virtual trials or ODR deliver a much speedier resolution, quicker even than the reasonable time within which justice requires that a case should be heard, then this may well offset the disappointment of not being vindicated in person. Further, and crucially, it may be that virtual courts and ODR will be confined to preliminary hearings and most final trials will be conducted in the traditional manner.

There may be a different concern—that a hearing or trial should be in a publicly accessible forum, so that any wrongdoer's acts are publicly declared and denounced. This could clearly be achieved across the Internet in the case of virtual courts but it is less obvious how ODR could be publicly viewed. Interestingly, this concern could equally be a call for televising or broadcasting hearings, which would render them radically more public. This is already happening. Around 90,000 people each day are reported to view the proceedings of the UK Supreme Court, live on the Sky News website.

As to the actual fairness of decisions, there is no obvious reason why judges or online mediators should be any less impartial, independent, or just when physically remote from some or all litigants, witnesses, and lawyers. It will of course be crucial, in the pursuit of fairness, that there is no actual difference between the soundness of decisions and findings delivered online and those that flow from conventional hearings.

Other important questions abound. What about the reliability and credibility of evidence taken remotely? Will judges, juries, and lawyers be at a disadvantage if they cannot look across the courtroom directly into the eyes of witnesses? Or will close-up, three-dimensional video on large, high-resolution monitors permit improved scrutiny? Should lawyers, in virtual trials, be with their clients at the camera-end of proceedings or in the hearing rooms near the judges? If the experience of giving evidence remotely is, as is likely, less intimidating than being in a physical courtroom, will this be conducive to evidence that is more or less convincing or decisions that are more or less authoritative and well founded?

More generally, flowing from the thinking of Judith Resnik and Dennis Curtis—in their magisterial book, *Representing Justice*—what will be the impact of public perceptions of justice, if one of its main icons, the courtroom, is displaced? Could well-designed ODR indeed become symbolic of a new, more inclusive era for dispute resolution? While virtual trials and ODR may seem alien or outlandish for policymakers and opinion formers of today, few of these individuals hail from the Internet generation. Future generations, for whom working and socializing online will be second nature, may feel very differently. Indeed, for tomorrow's clients, virtual hearings and ODR together may improve access to justice and offer routes to dispute resolution where none would otherwise be available.

It is too early to answer many of the questions just posed in a conclusive way. No doubt, more empirical research and analysis are needed. But, on the face of it, there are no knockdown objections, no overriding concerns of law or principle, that should call a halt to the ongoing and advanced computerization of courts.

And so, although the current advances may seem modest and faltering, I predict that e-working, IT-enabled courts, virtual courts, and ODR will come to dominate dispute resolution in the future. That is the world into which tomorrow's lawyers are striding.

PART THREE

Prospects for Young Lawyers

11 | New Jobs for Lawyers

In years to come, I predict that conventional lawyers will not be as prominent in society as today. Clients will not be inclined to pay expensive legal advisers for work that can be undertaken by less expert people, supported by smart systems and standard processes. This prediction does not signal the end of lawyers entirely, but it does point to a need for fewer traditional lawyers. At the same time, when systems and processes play a more central role in law, this opens up the possibility of important new forms of legal service, and of exciting new jobs for those lawyers who are sufficiently flexible, open-minded, and entrepreneurial to adapt to changing market conditions.

The Expert Trusted Adviser

Two kinds of traditional lawyer will, however, still be in play for the foreseeable future. When work cannot be standardized or computerized, and bespoke service is unavoidable, clients will still call upon their 'expert trusted advisers'. These are intelligent, creative, innovative lawyers who can fashion and articulate new solutions and strategies for clients who have complex or high-value legal challenges (the expert element). These are also lawyers who can communicate their guidance not just with integrity and in a confidential manner but in a highly tailored, customized, and personalized way (the trusted component). Many lawyers will say that this is precisely what they do today. They will tell you that all their work already requires expert and trusted handling. Clients think otherwise. In the end, those who handcraft while their competitors are able to source their services in alternative, reliable, and less costly ways will quickly fail to be in demand.

The Enhanced Practitioner

There will also be a need for the 'enhanced practitioner', a skilled, knowledgeable but not deeply expert lawyer, who will not be asked to deliver a bespoke service but, enhanced by modern techniques of standardization and computerization, will work further to the right-hand side of the evolutionary path that I describe in Chapter 3. The enhanced practitioner will often act as a legal assistant to the expert trusted adviser, for those tasks that require a lawyer but not necessarily a costly specialist. Again, though, the market will only have appetite for these kinds of assistant or associate when their legal experience is genuinely needed.

Although the long-term prospects for most conventional lawyers are much more limited than in the past, I urge young lawyers not to be de-motivated or downhearted, because there will be, I believe, a promising range of new opportunities and new careers for people trained in the law. I summarize these in Table 11.1.

TABLE 11.1. New jobs for lawyers

the legal knowledge engineer
the legal technologist
the legal hybrid
the legal process analyst
the legal project manager
the ODR practitioner
the legal management consultant
the legal risk manager

I am sure there will be others, but these are the jobs that flow quite clearly from the arguments and claims of this book.

The Legal Knowledge Engineer

When legal service comes to be standardized and computerized, talented lawyers will be required in great numbers to organize and model huge quantities of complex legal materials and processes. The law will need to be analysed, distilled, and then captured as standard working practices and embodied in computer systems. The result of this might be, for example, an online legal service, or it could be that the law is seamlessly embedded in some broader system or process (see Chapter 5).

Developing legal standards and procedures, and organizing and representing legal knowledge in computer systems, is irreducibly a job of legal research and legal analysis. More than this, it is often more intellectually demanding than traditional legal work, largely because it is more taxing to create a system that can solve many problems than to find an answer to a specific issue.

It is plainly wrong to imagine, as many conventional lawyers do, that the development of standards and systems is a task that can be handed over to junior lawyers, professional support staff, or even systems analysts. If a modern legal business intends to compete on the strength of its first-rate standards and systems, then it must have first-rate lawyers engaged in building them. These lawyers will be legal knowledge engineers.

The Legal Technologist

The practice of law and the administration of justice have become massively dependent on information technology and the Internet. When legal service becomes impractical or unimaginable without IT, it is vital to have experienced and skilled individuals who can bridge the gap between law and technology. Until recently, two groups populated the world of legal technology. The first was made up of mainstream technologists who found their way into legal environments and did their best to understand the mysterious ways of lawyers, courts, and clients. The other camp was occupied by lawyers with a fascination for computers—some were mere hobbyists, while others attained a more profound appreciation of the world of IT. But neither group, generally, was populated by professional legal technologists, individuals trained and experienced both in the practice of law and in the profession of systems engineering and IT management. While the technologists and hobbyists worked well enough when IT was largely at the periphery of the delivery of services to clients, we now need a new breed of able and credentialed legal technologists to help to take the legal profession fully into the 21st century. No longer will it suffice to have mere interpreters, who explain technology matters to lawyers and legal matters to technologists. We require a new cadre of self-sufficient legal technologists whose impact on modern society will be profound—they will build the foundations upon which legal service is built and the channels through which non-lawyers can access the law.

The Legal Hybrid

Lawyers of the future will need to diversify to stay in business. If it is accepted that traditional service will become less common, then I expect lawyers to extend their capabilities by becoming increasingly multidisciplinary. Many lawyers already assert that they are insightful in neighbouring disciplines, and already act, for example, as strategists, management consultants, business advisers, market experts, deal brokers, organizational psychologists, and the rest. Often, with a little probing, it transpires that their experience has been picked up through a brief course or by dipping into an introductory textbook. Although some lawyers like to think otherwise, it is not generally possible to take on a new discipline in 72 hours. Lawyers are highly intelligent human beings (by and large) who are undoubtedly capable of broadening their domains of expertise and becoming first-rate hybrid advisers. But if commercial lawyers want to be strategy consultants, if corporate lawyers aspire to be deal brokers, and if family lawyers wish to be psychologists—and I strongly support this diversification—then this must be supported by comprehensive and rigorous training that they undertake willingly. The legal hybrids of tomorrow will be formidably schooled and unarguably expert in their related disciplines and, in turn, will be able to add considerable value to the legal services they offer to clients.

The Legal Process Analyst

I have spoken rather glibly in this book, especially in Chapter 4, about decomposing deals and disputes into their constituent tasks and sourcing these tasks through a multitude of providers. However, the job of analysing a piece of legal work, subdividing the assignment into meaningful and manageable chunks, and identifying the most appropriate supplier of services for each, is itself a task that requires deep legal insight and experience. This will not be an occupation for business or systems analysts. It is a job for what I call 'the legal process analyst'. This individual will often be employed within an in-house legal department, for it is not unreasonable for organizations to expect their internal lawyers to be expert at identifying the most efficient and effective way of handling their legal work. Alternatively, legal process analysis could be a service offered by law firms or other third party providers such as accounting firms or legal process outsourcers. Today, there are very few legal process analysts but they are already in demand. Most of the major law firms and in-house legal departments with which I work are very clear that they would readily engage the services of individuals who could undertake reliable, insightful, rigorous, and informed analysis of their central legal processes.

The Legal Project Manager

Once the work of the legal process analyst is done, the deal or dispute that has been decomposed and prepared for multi-sourcing will not look after itself. To ensure the success of multi-sourcing, the legal market will require what I call 'the legal project manager'. When the legal process analyst has completed the specification (decomposition and proposed multi-sourcing) it is the job of the legal project manager to allocate work to a selection of appropriate providers, to ensure they complete their decomposed work packages on time and to budget, to control the quality of the various packages, to oversee and supervise the output and delivery, and to pull the various work packages together into one seamless service for the client. This is similar in many ways to the role of the production manager in a manufacturing environment.

The discipline of legal project management should, in my view, be built upon theory and experience from related management disciplines, such as logistics and supply-chain management. No doubt, the legal sector will come to develop its own sophisticated tools and techniques, such as 'legal supply-chain management' and 'legal logistics', which will be core subjects in future courses on legal project management.

The ODR Practitioner

With the advent of online dispute resolution (ODR—see Chapter 10) as a common mechanism for the settling of disagreements, there will be call for practitioners in this emerging field. These specialists will advise clients on how best to use ODR facilities and will be experts in resolving disputes conducted in electronic environments. It is very early days for services such as e-negotiation and e-mediation, but I have little doubt that imaginative lawyers will, over time, become superior users of these systems and will devise ingenious new techniques that will bestow advantage on those they guide. Litigators need not appear in courtrooms or even in virtual hearing rooms to add value. But they will need to build a new set of skills and methods which position their clients who are involved in ODR in a demonstrably better position than if they use these systems on their own. New careers will also open up for e-negotiators and e-mediators, those individuals whose intervention and adjudication will actually be required in the ODR process. Here, as elsewhere in this chapter, the competences that are called for will extend beyond expertise in black-letter law.

The Legal Management Consultant

Many in-house legal departments face a wide variety of management challenges (including, for instance, strategy formulation, team building, know-how development, and the introduction of information technology). And yet most General Counsel and in-house lawyers have little experience of management issues and so often seek external help. Today, some law firms offer guidance on various management issues, but they generally do so in an ad hoc and reactive fashion. Less frequently, professional management consultants are brought in. Given the considerable experience that many law firms have of management issues that arise in their own legal businesses, it is often suggested that these firms might set up their own full-time consulting practices to advise in-house legal departments. The English law firm Eversheds has done precisely this, and is already enjoying success and receiving plaudits. And there is persuasive precedent elsewhere for such a move: in the world of the 'Big 4' accounting firms, their consulting practices originally grew out of their audit businesses; while, more recently, tax management consultancy practices have been built on the back of the work of traditional tax firms.

While the market for this kind of legal management consultancy is still in its youth, it is likely to grow steadily, not just as a way of law firms adding value to their conventional services but as a service line in its own right. Likely services include strategy consulting (on issues such as long-term planning, alternative sourcing, organizational structure, value-chain analysis of in-house departments, and legal needs assessment) and operational or management consulting (for example, on recruitment, selection of law firms, panel management, financial control, internal communications, and document management).

Additionally, some legal management consulting providers will offer legal process analysis services. I do not believe that these services can easily or intuitively be provided by lawyers on an informal basis. Instead, legal management consulting will emerge as a discipline in its own right.

The Legal Risk Manager

My final category of lawyer for the future is perhaps the most urgently needed and longest overdue. As is noted in Chapter 7, most General Counsel consider their primary responsibility to be that of legal risk management. This comes through overwhelmingly in the research I have undertaken in the last decade within the in-house legal community. General Counsel, like the boards to which they report, have a strong preference for avoiding legal problems rather than resolving them. They prefer, as said before, a fence at the top of the cliff to an ambulance at the bottom. What is striking, however, is that there is scarcely a law firm in the world that has acknowledged this need and developed a sophisticated range of processes, methodologies, techniques, or systems to help their clients identify, assess, quantify, hedge, monitor, and control the plethora of risks that confront them. I expect this to change, and the agents of change will be the professional legal risk managers. Whereas conventional legal service is reactive in nature, by which I mean that lawyers (in firms and in-house) spend most of their time responding to questions put to them by their clients, legal risk managers will be proactive. Their focus will be on anticipating the needs of those they advise, on containing and pre-empting legal problems. Their preoccupation will not be with specific deals and disputes but with potential pitfalls and threats to the business. Legal risk managers will undertake jobs such as legal risk reviews, litigation readiness assessments, compliance audits, and analysis of contractual commitments. Talented legal risk managers will be lawyers with insight into the discipline of risk management and will draw also on techniques from strategy consulting. This will not be a side-show for the legal profession. It will fundamentally alter the way that clients administer their legal affairs. And the best legal risk managers may, in due course, be eligible for the much wider corporate role of chief risk officer.

Twist to the Tale

Taken together, the eight new jobs I have identified for tomorrow's lawyers will provide a rich and exciting new set of career opportunities for those who aspire to work in the law for many decades yet. I accept that these jobs are not those that law students generally have in mind when embarking upon law school. But they will be intellectually stimulating and socially significant occupations nonetheless. I know that some lawyers, when they hear of these new jobs, tend to regard them as less prestigious and worthy than traditional consultative service (many craftsmen no doubt felt similarly when their work was industrialized). I can only respond by saying that those who are already involved in these new roles do consider them rewarding and challenging. Many find themselves contributing in a different but still meaningful way to the higher ideal of an improved justice system.

There is a twist to this tale, however. My guidance to aspiring lawyers who are keen to work in one or more of the eight jobs is that it still makes sense, in the first instance, to qualify as a conventional lawyer. This may not be necessary but I think it desirable, not simply because it will for many years yet be useful to enjoy the status of being, say, a qualified solicitor or barrister, but because exposure to and understanding of traditional legal service should provide a valuable foundation upon which to build any new career in law. I am not suggesting that it will not be possible for a law graduate to become a first-rate legal knowledge engineer or legal project manager without having practised as a lawyer. But I do think it would be helpful to have the experience of mainstream legal work.

Lawyers in training should be proactive, however; always on the lookout for experiences that prepare them for tomorrow. I particularly recommend being seconded to clients, working in a variety of countries, and keeping close to the firm's technological developments.

All of that said, I know how difficult it is for many law graduates, in 2012, to secure training contracts and pupillages. This leads, then, to another question: whether as a conventional lawyer or in one of the new legal jobs, who will employ you in the future?

12 | Who Will Employ Young Lawyers?

Sceptics may regard my list of projected law jobs in the last chapter as rather fanciful, not least because they cannot imagine today's law firms or in-house legal departments creating and offering the new roles that I describe.

The mistake here is to think that these new jobs will always be grafted onto old legal businesses. This is not how events are likely to unfold. It is more likely that many of these new roles will be offered by a new range of employers who will work in quite different types of legal business. This will be enabled by liberalization (see Chapter 1) and driven by growing acceptance that many legal tasks no longer require the direct involvement of traditional lawyers. It is not that law firms cannot or will not create the new jobs, but that to do so will often disrupt their conventional businesses. It will simply be easier for new careers and occupations to be fashioned by those businesses, as summarized in Table 12.1 (overleaf), that are currently able to design their future legal services strategy on a blank sheet of paper.

TABLE 12.1. Tomorrow's employers

global accounting firms
major legal publishers
legal know-how providers
legal process outsourcers
High Street retail businesses
legal leasing agencies
new-look law firms
online legal service providers
legal management consultancies

The Return of the Global Accounting Firms

Most young and aspiring lawyers will not remember the foray of the big accounting firms into the legal market in the early 2000s. The most ambitious of these was Andersen Legal, the legal network of Arthur Andersen, then one of the world's largest accounting and tax practices. At its peak, Andersen Legal had a presence in 30 countries and a total number of lawyers of 2,500. This made it the ninth largest law firm in the world (by revenue). It was growing rapidly, both in size and reputation. Its brand was strong and its multidisciplinary objectives appealed to many clients. It offered a dynamic and exciting working environment, and in my view (biased perhaps, because I was one of their advisers) looked set to redefine the legal market.

Remarkably, Andersen Legal died. Contrary to the common view, however, it did not fail because of some fundamental defect of strategy or business model. Rather, Andersen Legal's demise was a direct consequence of the collapse in 2001 of a giant American corporation called Enron and, in turn, the remarkable implosion of the legal network's parent organization, Arthur Andersen (who were external auditors while Enron perpetrated various accounting frauds). The Andersen debacle did not establish that accounting firms could not provide legal services, although there did follow new bodies of regulations that prohibited these firms from providing other professional services to their audit clients. And this was a notable deterrent for accounting firms which were contemplating the continuation of their legal services. But it was not, and is not, a blanket and definitive prohibition.

In any event, I predict that the 'Big 4' (Deloitte, KPMG, PwC, and Ernst & Young) will soon be back in the legal profession. In fact they have never left and most of them, particularly in continental Europe, already enjoy several hundred million pounds worth of annual fee income from the legal services that are offered in conjunction with their tax work. Although liberalization is often said to be a catalyst or justification for their return to the law, the more likely attraction is that the legal market, as this book stresses, is a market of immense value and yet is one in a great state of flux. The accounting firms see this as a time of great opportunity—they believe they are well equipped to help meet the clients' more-for-less challenge.

Their strategies for re-entering the legal market are not yet clear. On one view, they may not seek to compete directly for the bespoke work of the largest law firms. Instead, they may become an alternative legal provider, leading the way in such areas as legal process outsourcing, legal risk management, legal knowledge engineering, and computerization. Whatever competitive route they seek, these formidable and hugely resourced employers will provide a wide range of career opportunities for tomorrow's lawyers.

Major Legal Publishers

Two of the largest legal businesses in the world are Thomson Reuters and Reed Elsevier. These commercial giants have evolved from the production of conventional print-based publications to the provision of very large and popular legal databases (largely of primary source materials such as legislation and case law). But they have also diversified over the years and are clearly ambitious and acquisitive in the fields of legal technology, legal knowledge engineering, and online legal services. These businesses employ legions of lawyers and armies of software engineers. They are trusted suppliers to the legal profession, and they too see opportunity in the tumultuous legal world. They are commercially ambitious, high-tech, and experienced in carving out new market space. These businesses will, unquestionably, provide homes for many law graduates in the future. I think it unlikely that they will deliver conventional consultative advisory legal services but they will offer many of the other jobs noted in the previous chapter.

Legal Know-How Providers

Another dynamic class of potential employer for tomorrow's lawyers are legal know-how providers. Nimbler and more entrepreneurial than the major legal publishers, this category is typified by the English-based legal business known as PLC (Practical Law Company). This company has been growing steadily since the early 1990s, employs more than 200 lawyers, and operates extensively in England and the US. It provides a range of services to law firms and in-house lawyers, including legal research and updates, market intelligence, the provision of standard documents and practice notes, know-how, checklists and flow charts, alongside some conventional legal library services. The proposition to the market is that law firms and in-house departments that retain PLC do not themselves then need to maintain their own libraries, information and research services, or professional support lawyers.

Again, businesses such as PLC do not provide legal advice directly but they are engaged in many of the jobs outlined in Chapter 11. And it is easy to see, strategically, how they might progress to providing fuller ranges of legal knowledge engineering, legal process analysis, and legal project management services.

Another way of looking at such businesses is that they are alternative legal providers to which law firms and in-house lawyers will increasingly allocate decomposed tasks. And, as decomposition and multi-sourcing increase, so too will the commercial success and the number of employees of these legal know-how providers.

Legal Process Outsourcers

Perhaps the highest profile of the new, emerging, and alternative legal providers are the legal process outsourcers (LPOs), businesses that undertake routine and repetitive tasks such as document review in litigation and basic contract drafting. Typically, these businesses have established bases in countries in which labour costs are low, most notably in India. However, the LPOs also tend to have significant capabilities in the main jurisdictions in which their clients (law firms and in-house legal departments) are themselves located.

These third party outsourcers are ambitious, entrepreneurial concerns that have often grown rapidly from start-ups, and are unlikely to limit the scope of their services to their current boundaries. Thus, we can expect LPOs to undertake increasingly challenging (and not just the most routine) work, supported by ever more sophisticated processes and systems. And, as liberalization allows, some will doubtless position themselves to offer services that used to be the sole province of law firms.

LPOs are growing steadily, if not as rapidly as some overzealous commentators have projected. As suggested in Chapter 8, it is in the second stage of the evolution of the legal sector that I anticipate they will peak in their current form. But they too will no doubt adapt and evolve in response to market conditions.

LPOs will be interesting and rewarding employers for tomorrow's lawyers, especially those interested in legal knowledge engineering, legal process analysis, legal project management, and compliance process outsourcing.

High Street Retail Businesses

In England, the Co-operative Bank, now an 'alternative business structure' (an ABS—see Chapter 1), is already well positioned to deliver legal services from its network of High Street locations. For private clients (individuals as opposed to companies), securing legal services from a bank in the High Street may be more convenient and less forbidding than consulting a traditional law firm. More than this, however, as banks and other High Street businesses enter the legal market, they will bring standardization and computerization of routine work, especially high-volume, low-value work. These retail businesses will be direct competitors to traditional law firms, especially small firms, which will want to counter that their service is more personalized and therefore preferable. In the end, when the economy is tough, I expect the small firms will fail to compete on price.

While the intuition of many lawyers is to regard these new competitors as removing the need for lawyers, the reality is that the legal services provided by banks will need to be developed and often delivered by people of considerable legal experience. Although ABSs may well be funded and managed by non-lawyers, they will still employ lawyers, old and young. Here, as elsewhere, we should not anticipate that lawyers will no longer be needed; but recognize that tomorrow's lawyers may be engaged by quite different businesses. These businesses might be well-known High Street brands, such as those of banks, building societies, and supermarkets, but they might also be insurance companies (including legal expense insurers), financial advisers, or local accounting firms.

Legal Leasing Agencies

Another rapidly emerging home for lawyers are legal leasing agencies, the best known of which is Axiom. This is an international business, founded in the US, that offers an alternative career path for lawyers who do not wish to be employed within conventional law firms or in-house departments. For lawyers who want the flexibility to work perhaps six months of the year, such as those with young children, Axiom provides a home of sorts. They have built up a large pool of temporary lawyers who are prepared to work on a contract and project basis. The attraction for the client is that Axiom's lawyers can be placed within their organizations to meet urgent demands but will tend to cost about half of their equivalent in conventional law firms.

A few legal practices, most notably Berwin Leighton Paisner, with its Lawyers on Demand service, and Eversheds, with its Agile offering, have set up similar businesses that work alongside the traditional firms. Although providing these lawyers in parallel and at lower cost may be seen to cannibalize the firm's traditional work, as I always say of cannibalization—if it is going to happen, you should want to be one of the first to the feast. Thus, entrepreneurial law firms will see opportunities to make the legal experience of lawyers available in new and imaginative ways. For qualified lawyers who want to live a more flexible life, these legal leasing agencies will become increasingly important employers.

New-Look Law Firms

New-look law firms are also emerging in these changing times. The owners of legal businesses such as Clearspire in the US and radiant.law and Riverview Law in the UK have started their law firms afresh, and jettisoned the old business models. They do not seek to replicate the pyramidic profit structure, or to bill by the hour, or to work from expensive city buildings. Instead, they keep their overheads very low, they encourage home working, they have flexible resourcing models, they use IT and knowledge management imaginatively, they outsource their back-office functions, they employ paralegals, and all of this enables them to charge clients less and yet remain profitable.

These new-look law firms may not offer conventional career paths to partnership, and they may not be as profitable as young lawyers have come to expect of the top firms. But they will offer exciting, vibrant, and entrepreneurial environments in which many young lawyers will thrive in the future. These firms will be open to the overtures of young lawyers who come with ideas of how legal services might be revolutionized. It may even be that they will also be receptive to innovative ways of providing training contracts.

Conversations with new-look law firms tend to be different from interactions with traditional practices. They are less hidebound by past practices, more flexible, and more respectful, I expect, of ideas that emanate from lawyers who are young or young in heart.

Online Legal Service Providers

For young lawyers who are keen to pursue careers as legal knowledge engineers, a natural home may well be a provider of online legal services. Whether providing online advice, online production of documents, or online dispute resolution, these are businesses that analyse and pre-package the law, allowing clients (both consumers and businesses) to tap into legal insight and service without direct consultation with human lawyers. Deep legal expertise is required, however, in developing these systems and services, and many law graduates and young lawyers in the future will find employment in these businesses.

It is early days for online legal service, but it is hard to imagine, in an Internet-based world, that they will not gain considerable traction. The career opportunities here will vary enormously, from large-scale businesses which will seek, for example, to transform the production of legal documentation in complex deals, through to charitable organizations which will strive to increase access to justice in the ways discussed in Chapter 9.

Legal Management Consultancies

Some traditional consulting firms and some dedicated legal consulting practices will also provide employment for tomorrow's lawyers. These businesses will specialize, for example, in legal process analysis, legal project management, legal risk management, as well as in advising on the optimum way of managing and maintaining a sustainable internal legal function. These specialties may not look like the work that many young and aspiring lawyers have in mind when starting their study of law but they will be central to the legal market and to the interests of clients nonetheless.

In particular, the demand for legal process analysts and legal project managers will be considerable, so that young lawyers who have taken courses and profess experience in these fields may find themselves more employable than those who boast knowledge only of black-letter law.

Lawyers often speak disparagingly of management consultants. It is true that many advisers who claim to be consultants are less able or experienced than they claim. But there is also a very respectable and impressive body of management consultants whose methods and techniques, I hazard, will be those that many successful legal businesses embrace in years to come.

Your First Job in Law

If current trends continue, law students may find it increasingly difficult to secure traineeships or employment as young lawyers in conventional law firms. As I say in the previous chapter, if you are graduating from law school, I am still inclined to suggest (and will be for the next five or ten years) that you try to obtain work in a law firm or in-house legal department, so that you can complete your training and qualify as a lawyer. However, if you fail to do so—and this is one of my central and, I hope, positive messages—there will be many other legal businesses, as introduced in this chapter, which may well be interested in engaging you. Alternatively, if you are already qualified and are exploring your options beyond law firms, then exciting new businesses and new options are emerging.

13 | Training Lawyers for What?

L aw schools around the world are currently being criticized for accepting far more law students than will be employable in law firms and other legal businesses. In the US, for example, as Brian Tamanaha points out in his book, *Failing Law Schools*, government statistics establish that there will only be 25,000 new openings for young lawyers each year until 2018 while the law schools are annually producing around 45,000 graduates. For law students who have taken out enormous loans to undertake their legal studies, their anger is understandable. Some have even raised court actions against law schools for the refund of their tuition fees plus damages, arguing that there is an ongoing fraud in the legal education industry that threatens to leave a generation of law students in dire financial straits.

While these issues are of immense concern, my focus with law schools in this chapter is not on whether they are overselling and contributing to unemployment and great debt, but rather with the appropriateness of what these educational bodies actually teach. My interest is in whether law schools are adequately preparing law students for tomorrow's legal marketplace. In this connection, the current Legal Education and Training Review in England and Wales, the most thoroughgoing for 30 years, comes at a pivotal time. For me, the prime challenge is to articulate the education and training needs for the legal industry as it is likely to be, and not how it is today or was in the past.

Some Assumptions and Concerns

This is not the place for a detailed analysis and evaluation of educational theory and law. However, a number of assumptions and concerns underlie my views on the current and future training of lawyers, and I think it best to lay these out explicitly.

I assume, first, that the law can be an academic discipline worth pursuing for its own sake. There is a contrast, of course, between studying law at university in, say, England as opposed to the US because, in the former, this is usually undertaken in a first degree; whereas in the latter the learning of the law is generally undertaken in the form of graduate study. Accordingly, students in the US are more likely, when studying law, to be committed to the legal profession as a career.

When law is studied at an undergraduate level, it can be profoundly stimulating in its own right—here is one of humanity's most remarkable and sophisticated constructs, a comprehensive system of knowledge that provides a framework for human order and behaviour. To study the substantive rules themselves can be interesting, but to be immersed in subjects such as jurisprudence (broadly, the philosophy of law) and civil law (Roman law) can also be immensely rewarding as an intellectual pursuit. To agree that the academic study of law can be fulfilling in and of itself is emphatically not to suggest that law degrees should be devoted solely to matters of theory. Nor is it to concede that there is no place in a law degree for exposure to legal practice, or insight into the vocation of law, or the acquisition of some of the key skills of the practitioner.

My second assumption is that the training afforded by the pursuit of a law degree can provide useful skills and experience whether or not a career in law is later taken up. Historically, many students have gravitated towards accounting when seeking a broad training to serve them well for a career in the commercial world. But a legal training can also be extremely valuable—not just because law graduates have a grasp of a large body of rules and regulations, but for the intellectual rigour, the clarity of analysis, the precision with language, the facility for critical thought, the capacity for intensive research, and the confidence in public speaking that a good degree in law should build and provide.

At the same time, third, I am concerned that legal education, delivered in university and in professional exams and sufficient to lead to qualification, is less demanding than that required for many other respectable professions. I look at medicine, architecture, veterinary science, and generally see longer and more arduous courses of study. It is not that studying law at university and professional exams is a soft option, but it is certainly quicker and, at least arguably, easier to qualify as a lawyer than to gain entry into many of our other great professions.

My final issue is that the academic and practising branches of the legal profession are insufficiently dovetailed. I look with much admiration, and a little envy, at the great teaching hospitals in London, for example. There, under one roof, a professor of medicine will treat patients, train young doctors, and undertake research, often in the one day. In continental Europe there is a stronger tradition of university law professors also being in legal practice. But in England and to a large extent in the US and Canada, legal practitioners and legal scholars operate in different worlds. In some jurisdictions there is also an unhealthy disrespect in both directions: practising lawyers regard legal academics as ivory-towered theorists divorced from the real world, while legal scholars look upon the daily practice of law as mere business advice rather than serious and substantive black-letter enterprise.

In summary, if you are contemplating the study of law, I can assure you, if it is well taught, of a stimulating experience, which will equip you well for life. However, law schools can be criticized, and often are by practitioners, for not preparing young students adequately for the practice of law.

What Are We Training Young Lawyers to Become?

My critique of law schools so far has not touched on a far more fundamental concern. It is true that many practising lawyers question law graduates' preparedness for working in law firms. But if graduates are not well equipped for legal practice as currently offered, they are profoundly ill-prepared for the legal world of the next decade or two, as anticipated in the earlier parts of this book.

It therefore must be asked: what are we training large numbers of young lawyers to become? This is one of the most fundamental questions of the book. Are we schooling aspiring lawyers to become traditional one-to-one, solo, bespoke, face-to-face, consultative advisers who specialize in the black-letter law of individual jurisdictions and charge by the hour? Or are we preparing the next generation of lawyers to be more flexible, team-based, hybrid professionals, who are able to transcend legal boundaries, speak the language of the boardroom, and are motivated to draw on techniques of modern management and information technology? My profound concern is that the emphasis in law schools and professional training is overwhelmingly on the former, with little regard for the latter. Indeed, a more profound concern still is that many legal educators and policymakers do not even know there is a second option. My fear, in short, is that we are training young lawyers to become 20th-century lawyers and not 21st-century lawyers.

To look at this issue in another way, we are focusing, in the training of our lawyers, in the language of Chapter 11, on incubating a new generation of expert trusted advisers and enhanced practitioners but ignoring their likely future careers as legal knowledge engineers, legal technologists, legal process analysts, legal project managers, legal risk managers, and the rest.

It is, of course, vital that we continue to equip young lawyers with the wherewithal to function as first-rate expert trusted advisers and in-house practitioners, but, if curricula do not change, it will be neglectful of students and their clients of the future if we do not widen our training to encompass these other new roles.

In many law schools, the law is taught as it was in the 1970s, by professors who have little insight into or interest in the changing legal marketplace. Too often, scant attention is paid to phenomena such as globalization, commoditization, information technology, modern business management, risk assessment, decomposing, and alternative sourcing. And so, I stress again—if many law graduates in the UK are ill-prepared for legal work today, they are still less equipped for tomorrow.

Should we, therefore, extend the remit of law schools and colleges to include other disciplines such as risk management, project management, and legal knowledge management? Is there a place for the future in the busy law curriculum?

The Place for the Future in Legal Education

I am not for a second suggesting that we should jettison core legal subjects such as contract, constitutional law, and tort. Still less am I advocating that we no longer teach students about legal method—how to think like a lawyer, how to marshal and organize a complex set of facts, how to conduct legal research, how to reason with the law (deductively, inductively, analogically), how to interpret legislation and case law, and more. But we do need to think, across the life cycle of the training of young lawyers, how we can more adequately prepare them for legal practice in the coming decades.

It may be argued that the time and place to train law students in the new disciplines that I identify is not law school but in post-graduate courses, such as the legal practice courses and Bar professional training courses in England and Wales. And there may be a stronger argument still for more intensive training in these emerging fields in the law while undertaking a training contract, pupillage, or some kind of indenture or apprenticeship.

On balance, I do not think law schools can ignore future practice. Accordingly, I suggest that we should provide law students in law schools (and indeed at all stages of their education) at least with *options*, first, to study current and future trends in legal services; and, second, to learn some key 21st-century legal skills that will support future law jobs. I do not consider this unduly onerous for law schools; and so I think law students can reasonably demand this of those whom they are paying for the provision of sufficient and appropriate legal education. There is mounting evidence of the need for a legal profession that extends itself beyond traditional service to fields such as legal risk management and legal project management. I am making the case for no more than this: at all stages in the provision of legal education, students have the choice and opportunity to learn about their future and of being trained in these new skills and disciplines. Involving practitioners in the delivery of these optional courses would be good, both to give students insight into evolving experience in the market and to encourage cross-fertilization between the academic and practising branches of the profession. I suspect that these courses would be very well attended.

I also have an urgent request of law professors the world over: to take an interest in the future of legal service; to undertake research (perhaps socio-legal work) into trends in the profession; to expose students to the likely future; and to resist being (in the words of the Dean of a Canadian law school) at 'the cutting edge of tradition'. Law faculties around the world should instead follow the lead of innovators such as the University of Miami School of Law (whose LawWithoutWalls is an exciting, part-virtual, international initiative that aims to change the way that law is taught and practised), Michigan State University College of Law (whose 21st Century Law Practice Summer Program introduces students to the future of legal service), and Harvard Law School (whose Program on the Legal Profession is an admirable blend of research, teaching, and collaboration between academics and practitioners).

Finally, the line of thinking explored in this chapter also provides a new angle on an old question: 'If I want to be a lawyer, should I pursue a law degree as an undergraduate?' I offer no definitive response here but I can see, because tomorrow's legal service will increasingly draw on other fields, that there are stronger arguments now than in the past for studying other disciplines—such as management, computing, and systems analysis—prior to embarking on a legal career.

14 | Replacing the Old Training Ground

When I speak at conferences, I am invariably asked about the ways in which young lawyers will learn their trade in the future. The concern here is that, according to my hypothesis, a great deal of routine and repetitive work that used to be handled by young lawyers will soon be sourced in different ways, whether by legal process outsourcing, by paralegals, by computerization, or the rest. If the basic legal work, upon which young lawyers used to cut their teeth, is to be undertaken by others, how does a young lawyer take the early steps towards becoming an expert?

A Training Problem

This is an important but not fatal challenge to those who advocate alternative sourcing. It is not fatal, in part because this is an obstacle with which very few clients have sympathy. In essence, what we have here is a training problem—alternative sourcing requires law firms to rethink the way they train their lawyers. And most clients, if given the choice, will choose lower-cost legal service from a law firm that has to overhaul its training over a high price service from a firm that seems intransigently wedded to training methods of the past.

The root of the problem here is that, because of the so-called 'war for talent', many firms pay very large salaries to attract the most gifted graduates. However, no matter how talented these trainees and aspiring young lawyers might be, their value for the first couple of years in law offices lies more in their potential than in the actual services they can deliver to clients. Until around 2006 the unspoken truth was that most clients paid for the training of law firms' aspiring young lawyers. The clients were charged at fairly high hourly rates for the work of these trainees, even though much of the work was process-based and the young lawyers were learning on the job. They may have been quick learners but they had insufficient experience or expertise to justify the rates at which they were being charged. Today, in contrast, in more austere times, when clients are demanding more legal service at less cost, they are no longer tolerant of paying for the time of budding lawyers who are learning their trade by working on their clients' deals and disputes.

Some years ago, when pondering these issues, I decided to interview some trainee solicitors to determine their take on this conundrum. I spoke to aspiring lawyers who were reviewing endless boxes of documents in preparation for litigation and others who were undertaking major due diligence exercises in support of large deals. I asked them how they would learn their trade if the work they were currently doing was to be, say, outsourced to India. Uniformly they responded that it took only a few hours to learn how to work through piles of documents, and not several months. To express this point more provocatively, we should not confuse training with exploitation. It is disingenuous to suggest that young lawyers are asked to undertake routine legal work largely as a way of them learning their trade. Rather, this delegation has been one mainstay in supporting the pyramidic model of profitability that has enjoyed such unchallenged success until recently.

In any event, it is not at all obvious that aspiring lawyers become expert lawyers by spending months on what is largely administrative work. There is greater evidence that young lawyers learn their trade by working closely with, and observing, legal experts in action.

That said, I do recognize that some work that might be alternatively sourced provides a useful training ground. But it is far from clear how law firms might respond to clients' new-found distaste for being charged for the training of their supplier's young people. One likely option, although challenging for many firms, would be no longer to charge clients for trainees and young lawyers unless and until they genuinely bring value. This would directly reduce the profit of those firms that rely on the pyramidic structure. Two possible consequences might follow for young lawyers. The first is that, with the exception of the supremely talented, young lawyers might come to get paid less in their early years of working in law firms than in the past. The second is that law firms are likely to recruit young and aspiring lawyers in smaller numbers. This does not necessarily mean that all young lawyers will be less employable, because there will be new jobs for lawyers and new employers to work with (see Chapters 11 and 12). But for law graduates, this does indeed appear to be threatening.

Re-Thinking Legal Training

What is the alternative to training lawyers by putting them to work on relatively straightforward and routine legal matters?

If law firms are genuinely committed to training, I suggest that it should be founded on three basic building blocks in the future. The first is a reversion to some variant of the apprenticeship model. Once young lawyers have their paper qualifications, research and experience suggest that working closely alongside experienced lawyers is a powerful and stimulating way of learning how to move from the law in books to the law in action. If young lawyers are able to share a room with a seasoned practitioner or, as works very well in large accounting firms, to work in open-plan areas with experienced professionals, they will observe and learn, at first-hand, effective methods for communicating with and serving clients. If they instead spend most of their time only with other young lawyers and with large boxes of documents, they are less likely to witness and absorb best practice.

Second, it may be that, when significant bodies of work are sourced from beyond the firm, young lawyers may nevertheless, in parallel, undertake samples of this work, partly to learn their trade and partly perhaps as a way of quality controlling the work done by external providers. In contrast with the past, law firms would need themselves to bear the cost of this work.

Finally, young lawyers should benefit from existing and emerging techniques of e-learning, which in their most advanced forms can be tremendously powerful. This extends beyond online lectures (which themselves can be useful) to online simulated legal practice and virtual legal learning environments. The legal profession's adoption of technology should extend beyond office automation and client service into the way in which we educate and train our young lawyers.

e-Learning and Simulated Legal Practice

Most senior lawyers and judges of today were legally educated before the birth of the personal computer. Lectures, tutorials, and countless hours in dusty law libraries were the order of the day. And much of the time was spent memorizing vast lists of case names and sections of statutes, alongside potted summaries of their significance. None of this should be uncritically inherited by tomorrow's law schools and by the colleges that offer conversion and legal practice courses.

Take traditional one-hour lectures as an example. There are now compelling arguments, based on cost and on the reality of what actually goes on in a lecture theatre, for reserving conventional live lectures for the relatively rare occasions when wonderful speakers are scheduled and expected to deliver a memorable social or educational experience. Here is the truth about most conventional law lectures in the UK—they are often not given by gifted (or even trained) orators. Some professors mumble and ramble, others simply read from their notes, while only a very few are inspirational. No wonder the attendance is low. And this phenomenon persists across the country in countless law schools. It is wasteful and insufficiently edifying. There is no good reason for not replacing the ramblers and the dictators by online lectures, which can be presented by wonderful and inspirational speakers (selected from across the land) who make webcasts of their lectures available. Anyone who has used TED (<http://www.ted.com>)

will know how powerful an online lecture can be. Alternatively, live lectures of a sort can be given as real-time webinars, which allow students to participate and debate throughout.

In 2009, I was asked to undertake a five-year review of e-learning at the College of Law in England. I found that electronic tutorials and online supervision had changed the learning experience of law students on the college's legal practice course. More than 400 'i-tutorials' had been developed—online, 'head and shoulders', webcasts by legal experts with slides on the side. Students found these mini-lectures highly convenient in that they could be stopped, started, and replayed, on hand-held devices as well as on laptops. The college went a step further and developed one-to-one supervision by tutors, conducted virtually rather than face to face. This created what I called an 'electronic Oxbridge'—many of the strengths of the traditional tutorial system were secured (the pressure, the inspiration, and the attention of a personal expert tutor) but achieved in a practical, affordable way.

Online lectures, i-tutorials, and virtual supervision are only part of the future for legal education. The pioneering work of Paul Maharg moves us beyond this first generation into a world of simulation-based training and transactional learning, as described in his book, *Transforming Legal Education*. He pioneered these techniques in the post-graduate Scottish Diploma of Legal Practice taught at Strathclyde University for which he designed a fictional town, 'Ardcalloch', in which law students play the role of lawyers in virtual law firms. A little like a legal *Second Life*, the students practise law—simulations of actual legal transactions and disputes—with experienced solicitors acting as clients and judges in this virtual environment. All sorts of facilities are made available online: virtual offices, various institutions, professional networks, and with a collection of documentary resources to lend authenticity, including newspaper clippings, photographs, wills, bank books, and advertisements. I have no doubt that students immersed in such a simulated working environment, with practising lawyers participating and supporting, are exposed to a more profound and memorable learning experience, that greatly outstrips ill-attended lectures and non-participative tutorials.

These e-learning techniques will only become more powerful—simulated advocacy, drafting, client meetings, negotiations, document reviews, due diligence exercises, and much more will increasingly be available online. These facilities will be immeasurably more effective in training young lawyers than asking them to review endless piles of documents or memorize lists of cases. And they will go some considerable way to patching the gaps left by alternative sourcing.

15 | Questions to Ask Employers

In this chapter, I change tense and emphasis. If you are a young or aspiring lawyer applying for a new job, I want now to equip you with some questions to pose when, at the end of a gruelling interview, you are faced with the inevitable query: 'Do you have anything you would like to ask us?' I also recommend these questions to you if you are a young lawyer wondering whether your current firm is one to which you should commit yourself in the long run. Note that these questions are very similar to those that I ask of law firm leaders when they engage me as an external consultant. Together, they seek to determine the depth of an organization's insight into the future and its appetite for change.

The questions come with a health warning. There are quite a few of them and, although it is good at a job interview to be engaged, savvy, and interested, I am not suggesting you fire off all of the queries at the one sitting. It is generally counter-productive at interviews to appear excessively objectionable or subversive. Also, I am conscious that the job market is so intensely competitive that many readers will be glad to secure any position at all, so that these questions might seem of peripheral concern. However, it is good to be armed with some penetrating observations and it should be helpful and relevant for tomorrow's lawyers to give serious thought to some difficult issues.

Do You Have a Long-Term Strategy?

This simple query can prompt all sorts of physical reactions, from nervous giggles to disparaging grunts. Law firm leaders often respond by claiming that they have not actually written down their strategy in a formal document but that all the partners know what their strategy is. Invariably, this is nonsense. In such firms, most partners will confess in private to having no clue as to the strategy of their business. The leaders themselves are either dissembling or rationalizing. It is not that a strategy document in and of itself has great value but an absence of such a document usually betrays an absence of strategic thinking.

Beware of law firm leaders who say that in the current economic climate their focus must be on the short term. The best leaders keep one eye on the short term and the other on the long-term strategic health of their organizations. Worry deeply if a senior partner is preoccupied with 'low-hanging fruit' or 'quick wins'. This frequently betrays short-termism which can precede rapid decline.

A quite different response is the production of a fat 300-page report. An external firm of management consultants will often have produced this. This of itself is problematic—the composition of the strategy of a firm, the document which seeks to determine its very future, is too important a task to outsource to another organization. Moreover, it should not take several hundred pages to articulate the strategy for a legal business.

You are unlikely ever to be handed a full strategy document, which will be guarded as though 'top secret'. But you may get a sanitized précis. What you should look for in this is evidence of a firm that has thought deeply about changes in the broader business environment and in the legal market in particular. There should be a sense from the document of the ambition of the firm, of where it hopes to be in, say, five years' time, and what major changes it must effect to get there. It should indicate the markets in which it intends to work and how it will seek to compete in these chosen markets. You should also find an indication of the values that are central to the firm, and of the culture it likes to engender. You should be convinced that the overall sense of strategic direction seems realistic. What to search for here is a relatively small number of major priorities, rather than a litany of piecemeal initiatives.

If a strategy document with such contents does not exist, then this is not a business that is preparing wisely for the future, and not a business, therefore, that is likely to provide a firm foundation for lawyers of tomorrow.

What Will Legal Service Look Like in 2035?

My previous question, about long-term strategy, is testing the business's view over perhaps the next five to ten years. This next query, about the way in which legal service might change over the next generation, is looking around 25 years out. In the introduction to this book, I observed that when I was at law school in the early 1980s and was discussing the future with my friends and professors, there seemed to be a shared view that the basic daily work of lawyers would be much the same a quarter of a century hence. In the event, we were not wrong. At that time, there were no obvious and imminent drivers of change, analogous to the more-for-less pressure, liberalization, and technology (the running themes of this book).

Looking at IT in particular, although IBM launched its PC when I was in the final year of my law degree, we did not yet live in a time of massive and foreseeable technological upheaval. In radical contrast, given that we are now witnessing an exponential increase in the uptake and power of technology, it would be remarkably shortsighted for anyone to maintain that legal service in, say, 2035, will be much the same as today. Of course, no one can predict what our world will be like then but in asking a prospective employer a question about the distant future, you should not be looking for a definitive, authoritative response. Indeed, be wary of anyone who is excessively dogmatic in any direction. The kind of firm in which you should want to build your career, if you are convinced by the arguments and predictions of this book, is a firm in which its members express both interest and concern about the years ahead. A dismissive response is a narrow-minded response, and you should be looking, in stark contrast, for a firm that is open-minded and welcoming of debate about possible futures.

Are You Comforted by Other Firms' Lack of Progress?

If change is unavoidable, then bright lawyers in impressive law firms will usually adapt promptly and effectively. They have no choice. If there is a burning platform of some sort, they have no option but to jump off. In the absence of such an imperative, most law firms, even the finest, tend to be driven more by a fear of lagging behind their competition than by a hunger for forging ahead of their rivals. Law firms, in other words, are motivated more by the need to avoid competitive disadvantage rather than a thirst for the attainment of competitive advantage. This is quite unlike many other sectors, such as consumer electronics, where the driving passion is to outpace and out-think the competition. When meeting with law firm leaders, I find the easiest way to motivate them is to speak of the notable achievements of their closest rivals.

It follows, therefore, that many lawyers do indeed derive great comfort from knowing that other firms, of whom they think highly, have made little attempt to rethink the way they work, or to embrace technology, or to take up many of the suggestions in this book.

Accordingly, you should view with great optimism a firm that insists that it is driven not by its competitors but by its clients' needs, that the market will clearly require fundamental changes, and that the conservatism of other firms presents an opportunity for a new market leader to emerge. If these are the messages that you hear from an organization, strive to gain employment with it.

Interestingly, if you meet with alternative providers in the legal marketplace, such as legal process outsourcers, legal publishers, or large accounting firms, then you will detect amongst them a far greater appetite for change, far greater excitement about the future, than that evinced by mainstream law firms in their often rather lacklustre response to shifting market conditions.

What are Your Preferred Approaches to Alternative Sourcing?

If this question is met with a blank expression or a whiff of incomprehension, it may need a little explaining, as follows: given that clients are increasingly asking their legal advisers to find ways of reducing the costs of routine and repetitive work, which approaches are you finding to be the most promising?

Treat with suspicion those firms that say no more than that they are looking very carefully at this challenge, or that they are currently in discussions with low-cost providers such as legal process outsourcers, contract lawyers, or the like. Look for evidence of action and activity rather than of reflection and discussion.

Even if firms say they have invested in some facility—perhaps a near-shore centre or subcontracting arrangement—probe a little further to test if this is tokenism or serious commitment. A number of firms do indeed have modest arrangements in place but these are often no more than gestures that allow the partners to say to clients that they are involved in some way.

Ordinarily, it will be clear if a firm is genuinely committed. You will sense their enthusiasm and they will have tales to tell about what has worked well and what needs further refinement.

What Role Will IT Play in Law Firms of the Future?

Most lawyers are not entirely comfortable in talking about the changing role of IT in their firms. They will speak articulately enough about the systems they currently use, such as email, word processing,

PowerPoint, and, of course, their beloved BlackBerry devices. Most law firms will have sophisticated IT departments and their dependence on technology is indeed profound. But the technologies I have in mind are not back-office systems but those that directly affect and support client services. One category, for example, is knowledge systems—the collection of applications (from intranets to databases) which seek to capture and make available a firm's collective experience and expertise; or client relationship systems, those services such as online deal rooms that provide new communication channels between firms and their clients; or online legal services—systems that provide legal advice and documents, for instance.

In the coming decade we will see information technology move out of the back-office and transform, often disruptively (see Chapter 5), the traditional way that lawyers have worked with their clients.

To gauge the technological sophistication of a firm that you are considering, you should look in the first instance for recognition of the kinds of change just described, and then for evidence of investment in these emerging technologies. One interesting sub-question to pose is: 'What is the formal process by which your firm monitors emerging technologies and evaluates their potential for your various practice areas?' You will find that very few firms have such a process. If you locate one that does, look no further.

Do You Have a Research and Development Capability?

If you are a consumer electronics company, like Apple or Sony, you have not yet invented the products that will be the foundations of your business in five years' time. The position is similar in pharmaceutical companies. This is why these and many other businesses have research and development (R&D) budgets and departments—teams of very bright people (that I envisage wearing white coats and having high brows) who are given freedom to think deeply and creatively and to come up with all sorts of possible offerings for the future. Most of their ideas never see the light of day. The R&D people are encouraged to think the unthinkable, to be bold and daring. And if their inventions are not commercialized, this is not regarded as failure.

There is an analogous challenge here for law firms. If what I say in Parts One and Two of this book come to pass, then lawyers too, perhaps five or ten years from now, will be offering services that they have not yet conceived. So, how are these firms going to innovate? Who is going to come up with new, market-changing legal services? It is not unreasonable to ask law firms whether they invest in R&D and, if so, in what way. A supplementary question here might be to ask what percentage of their annual fee income is ploughed back into an R&D budget (consumer electronics and pharmaceutical companies spend about 15 to 20 per cent of their turnover on R&D).

Very few firms currently have R&D budgets or departments, and so an encouraging reply would be that they know that this is soon going to be necessary. Firms that are dismissive and hope they can for some years squeeze yet more juice out of the old way of working should be viewed with some distrust as long-term places of employment.

If You Could Design a Law Firm From Scratch, What Would it be Like?

In my consulting work with clients, I have built a formal exercise around this question. I call it 'blank sheet thinking'. I have discovered that most lawyers, when thinking about the long term, tend to be contained and constrained by their current set-up. Their thinking ahead is legacy-based; they are walking backwards into the future. In contrast, in these times of great change, I encourage law firms to be vision-based, to put to one side the way their firms are currently organized and positioned, and take a leap forward to consider where they could and should be in five years' time.

To help them to engage in this vision-based thinking, I ask them to answer the following question: 'If you were given a blank sheet of paper and could design your practice or firm from scratch, what would it look like?' (I provide a series of prompts to support them but they need not detain us here.) Pursuing a similar line of inquiry, try to get a sense from your prospective employers of what would be different if they could wave a magic wand and, in response to current and impending pressures, were able to build their business afresh.

You may find, as I do, that this thought experiment releases lawyers from their focus on current ways of working and reveals some fascinating insights about where law firms might be located, how many people they would employ, how they would source their work, what technology they might deploy, the extent to which they would seek external capital, and much more.

If the upshot of the interviewers' responses to your questions is that their business would look much as the one they are managing today, then I would be deeply sceptical. On the other hand, if this question leads to a series of imaginative and engaging thoughts about different ways of working, then that employer may well be an exciting prospect for you.

Remember that I am not suggesting that you should bombard prospective employers with this last question *and* all the others outlined in this chapter. Nonetheless, it is impressive to be armed with a penetrating question or two; and the answers to the queries suggested here could be highly illuminating for your future.

16 | The Long Term

In the long run, the changes that I anticipate for lawyers and the administration of justice will be pervasive, irreversible, and transformational. I am not suggesting that this means the legal sector will be turned on its head over the next three to six months. But I am confident we will see some fundamental shifts over the next three to six years.

Looking further ahead, by 2035, to pick a date that will be mid-career for young lawyers of today, it is neither hyperbolic nor fanciful to expect that the legal profession will have changed beyond recognition. In this final chapter, my purpose is to put this legal revolution in some wider context.

Power Drills or Holes?

One of my favourite business stories concerns one of the world's leading manufacturers of power tools. It is said that this company takes all of its new executives on a training course when they join up, and at the outset a slide on a large screen is presented for their consideration. The slide is a photograph of a gleaming power drill and the trainers ask the assembled new recruits if this is what the company sells.

The new executives seem slightly surprised by this but together buck up the collective courage to concede that 'yes, this is indeed what the company sells'. With some evident satisfaction, the trainers ask for the next slide, which depicts a hole, neatly drilled in a piece of wood. 'This,' they say, 'is actually what our customers want, and it is your job as new executives to find ever more creative, imaginative, and competitive ways of giving our customers what they want.'

There is a great lesson here for lawyers. Most senior legal practitioners, when contemplating the future of their business, tend to be of power drill mentality. They ask themselves, 'What do we do today?' (answer: one-to-one, consultative advisory service, often billed on an hourly billing basis) and then, 'How can we make this service cheaper, quicker, or in some way better?' Very rarely do they take a step back and ask themselves, by analogy, about the hole in the wall in the legal world. What value, what benefits, do clients really seek when they instruct their lawyers?

For 20 years and more, I have been asking lawyers, 'What is the hole in the wall in the delivery of legal services?' One of best answers I have had came indirectly from KPMG, one of the world's leading accounting and tax firms. I am not a great fan of mission statements or the like, but on KPMG's website, some time ago, I noticed part of one that I thought was superb: 'we exist to turn our knowledge into value for the benefit of our clients'. I judge this to be a superb way of capturing the value that lawyers bring: lawyers have knowledge, expertise, experience, insight, and understanding that they can apply in the particular circumstances of their clients' affairs. Lawyers have knowledge and experience that their clients lack.

Notice that KPMG did not say that they exist to provide one-to-one consultative, advisory service on an hourly billing basis. They did not confuse their methods of working with the value they deliver.

Many insights flow from KPMG's rendition of the role of the professional or legal adviser. For lawyers, the most significant for me is a challenge that flows from it—what if we could find new, innovative ways of allowing our clients to tap into our knowledge and expertise? In particular, what if we, as lawyers, could make our knowledge and expertise available through a wide range of online legal services, whether for the drafting of documents or for the resolution of disputes? If we can find online methods of enabling access to our experience and the service is thereby less costly, less cumbersome, more convenient, and quicker, then I suggest that clients, oppressed as they are by the more-for-less challenge, would welcome these services with arms flung open. This, then, is the long term.

A New Legal Paradigm

It is often observed, not especially profoundly, that we cannot predict the future. This seems to give licence to the unimaginative, the short-sighted, and the indolent to discard any foresights as pointless speculation. In contrast, I join others who believe that we can anticipate many (but not all) broad trends, if not the specific details of the world yet to come.

One interesting way to think about the future is to contemplate the sustainability of what we currently have. Given our economic conditions, the shift towards liberalization, and the burgeoning, exponential increase in the power and uptake of information technology, I find it unimaginable that our current legal institutions and legal profession will remain substantially unchanged over the next decade. For much of the legal market, the model is not simply unsustainable; it is already broken.

Look at the law and legal service from another vantage point. At the heart of law and legal service is legal information (from raw law such as legislation through to deep expertise held in specialists' heads). Pause now and think about information. We are currently witnessing a change in the information sub-structure of society. This is the term I use to refer to the principal way in which information is captured, shared, and disseminated. I share the view of anthropologists who have observed that human beings have travelled through four stages of information sub-structure: the age of orality, where communication was dominated by speech; the era of script; then print; and now a world in which communication is increasingly enabled by information technology. There will no doubt be a fifth, when nanotechnology, robotics, genetics, and IT converge, perhaps in 30 or 40 years' time. My guess is—and I say this with some hesitation because it could easily be stripped from context by critics—that entire bodies of law and regulation will then be embedded in chips and networks that themselves will be implanted in our working practices or, eventually even, in or remotely accessible to our brains.

For now, we are coming to the end of the transitional phase between the third and fourth stages of development, between a print-based industrial society and an Internet-based information society. The key point here is that the information sub-structure in society determines to a large extent how much law we have, how complex it is, how regularly it changes, and those who are able, responsibly and knowledgeably, to advise upon it. If we examine the manner in which the law has evolved throughout history, we can understand the shifts in terms of changes in information sub-structure. At its core, then, law is information-based. And we are in the middle of an information revolution. It is not making a wild leap to suggest that the law and the work of lawyers will not emerge unchanged.

This thinking led me in 1996, in my book *The Future of Law*, to predict a shift in legal paradigm, by which I meant that many or most of our fundamental assumptions about legal service and legal process would be challenged and displaced by IT and the Internet. It was a 20-year prediction, so I can be called fully to account in 2016. I do not think I will be far out—when I look at IBM's Watson (see Chapter 1) and think of similar technology in law, or reflect on information retrieval systems that are already outperforming human beings engaged in document review, then I feel we are on the brink of a monumental shift.

Crucially, I concluded in 1996 that legal service would move from being a one-to-one, consultative, print-based advisory service to a one-to-many, packaged, Internet-based information service. I still think this—I believe it more strongly, in fact—and that is one premise upon which tomorrow's lawyers should build in planning for the long term.

Do We Need a Legal 'Profession'?

The changes I anticipate in this book raise further and deeper questions about the future of professional service. Why is it that we give monopoly rights to certain occupational groups over particular areas of human endeavour? The accountancy profession, medical profession, and the legal profession, for example, are exclusively entitled and permitted, respectively, to conduct statutory audits, to perform surgery, and to engage in advocacy in courtrooms. It is as though there is some social contract (unarticulated), which empowers certain skilled and knowledgeable classes of people to undertake work that it would be foolhardy or dangerous for lay people to attempt on their own. Thus, we have these trusted advisers, who are responsible for keeping their knowledge current and applying that knowledge in a confidential, affordable, and accessible way. We trust these individuals because of their training and experience, their competence and integrity, and their codes of conduct. And they enjoy the reputation and prestige of groups whose experience is respectfully called upon by fellow human beings.

There are, however, several problems with this model. In the first place, in most societies, we struggle to afford the delivery of professional knowledge and experience in a one-to-one, conventional manner. In these stressed economic times, health services, legal services, educational services, and many more are under enormous strain. The old model does not seem to yield readily affordable and accessible service.

The second challenge to the model is that a new channel for the delivery of knowledge and experience has been developed. This is the Internet. As indicated throughout this book, it is possible to allow lay people to tap into the insights and experience of lawyers through, for example, online legal guidance systems, automated document assembly systems, communities of legal experience, or even through less costly consultation by video conference.

A third challenge to the profession probes into the heart of a crucial issue—the motivation of those who are in opposition to change. Building on Clay Shirky's quotation at the start of this book, it is leaders as well as institutions within professions who try to preserve the problem to which they are the solution. In more common parlance, turkeys rarely step forward to vote for an early Christmas. There are none so conservative or reactionary as those who benefit from the status quo. It is no doubt this line of thinking that led George Bernard Shaw famously to claim that 'all professions are conspiracies against the laity'.

I put it a little differently. I observe, in law, that there are two distinct camps (and a few in between): the benevolent custodians and the jealous guards. The benevolent custodians are those who, consistent with the conception of professionalism just noted, regard it as their duty to nurture the law and make it affordable and accessible to members of society. They are the interface between lay people and the law and they strive to be user-friendly. In contrast, the jealous guards wish to ring-fence areas of legal practice and make it their exclusive preserve, whether or not the activity genuinely requires the experience of lawyers and with little regard to the impact of this quasi-protectionism on the affordability and availability of legal service. In the US, when lawyers object to online legal services that help citizens and claim the providers are engaged in the unauthorized practice of law, we frequently see this second camp in action. The disingenuity of their claims—that their primary concern is access to justice or safeguarding the interests of their clients—makes me shudder. In truth, for many (but not all), their primary concern is themselves and threats to their income and their self-esteem.

Your Mission

I implore you, tomorrow's lawyers, to take up the mantle of the benevolent custodians; to be honest with yourselves and with society about those areas of legal endeavour that genuinely must be preserved for lawyers in the interests of clients. But you should work in the law in the interests of society and not of lawyers. Where, in all conscience, legal services can responsibly and reliably be offered by non-lawyers, celebrate access to justice and draw upon your creative and entrepreneurial talents to find other ways that your legal knowledge and experience can bring unique value to your clients.

As I often remind lawyers, the law is no more there to provide a living for lawyers than ill health exists to offer a livelihood for doctors. It is not the purpose of law to keep lawyers in business. The purpose of lawyers is to help to support society's needs of the law.

Alan Kay, a computer scientist from Silicon Valley, makes a different but related point. He once said that 'the best way to predict the future is to invent it'. This is a powerful message for tomorrow's lawyers. The future of legal service is not already out there, in some sense pre-articulated and just waiting to unfold. It is not that I, and other commentators who follow trends in legal services, can see the future where most lawyers cannot. All that I do is lay out a metaphorical buffet—a set of possible courses that lawyers and other legal service providers may or may not choose.

Here is the great excitement for tomorrow's lawyers. As never before, there is an opportunity to be involved in shaping the next generation of legal services. You will find most senior lawyers to be of little guidance in this quest. Your elders will tend to be cautious, protective, conservative, if not reactionary. They will resist change and will often want to hang on to their traditional ways of working, even if they are well past their sell-by date.

In truth, you are on your own. I urge you to forge new paths for the law, our most important social institution.

FURTHER READING

There is a rapidly growing literature on the future of legal services. In the short bibliography here, I include the publications explicitly mentioned in the main body of the book together with a selection of texts and longer articles that I recommend to readers who want to delve further into the field. At the end, I also note a few online resources that I find invaluable: in each case, the name of the author is provided, along with a paraphrase of their own descriptions of these blogs. I have not included references for all law firms, legal businesses, and online services referred to in the book: they can easily be found online.

Publications

Baker, S., *Final Jeopardy: Man vs. Machine and the Quest to Know Everything* (New York: Houghton Mifflin Harcourt, 2011).

Benkler, Y., *The Wealth of Networks* (New Haven: Yale University Press, 2006).

Black, N., *Cloud Computing for Lawyers* (Chicago: American Bar Association, 2012).

Bull, C., *The Legal Process Improvement Toolkit* (London: Ark, 2012).

Christensen, C., *The Innovator's Dilemma* (Boston: Harvard Business School Press, 1997).

Dershowitz, A., *Letters to a Young Lawyer* (New York: Basic Books, 2001).

Dutton, W. and Blank, G., *Next Generation Users: The Internet in Britain*, Oxford Internet Study 2011 (Oxford: Oxford Internet Institute, 2011).

Faure, T., *The Smarter Legal Model* (London: The Practical Law Company, 2010).

Galbenski, D., *Unbound: How Entrepreneurship is Dramatically Transforming Legal Services Today* (Royal Oak: Lumen Legal, 2009).

Grossman, M. and Cormack, G., 'Technology-Assisted Review in E-Discovery Can be More Effective and More Efficient Than Exhaustive Manual Review' (2011) XVII(3) *Richmond Journal of Law and Technology* 1.

Kafka, F., *The Trial* (Harmondsworth: Penguin, 1983).

Kimbro, S., *Limited Scope Legal Services: Unbundling and the Self-Help Client* (Chicago: American Bar Association, 2012).

Kowalski, M., *Avoiding Extinction: Reimagining Legal Services for the 21st Century* (Chicago: American Bar Association, 2012).

Kurzweil, R., *The Singularity is Near* (New York: Viking, 2005).

Legal Services Board, *Understanding Consumer Needs from Legal Information Sources* (London: LSB, 2012).

Levitt, T., 'Production-Line Approach to Service' (1972) *Harvard Business Review* (September–October) 41–52.

Levitt, T., *Marketing Myopia* (Boston: Harvard Business School Publishing Corporation, 2008).

Levy, S., *Legal Project Management* (Seattle: DayPack, 2009).

Lightfoot, C., *The Naked Lawyer* (London: Ark, 2010).

Maharg, P., *Transforming Legal Education* (Aldershot: Ashgate, 2007).

Ministry of Justice, *Virtual Court Pilot: Outcome Evaluation* (London: Ministry of Justice, 2010), available at <http://www.justice.gov.uk/>.

Morgan, T., *The Vanishing American Lawyer* (New York: Oxford University Press, 2010).

Mountain, D.R., 'Disrupting Conventional Law Firm Business Models Using Document Assembly' (2007) 15(2) *International Journal of Law and Information Technology* 170–91.

Paliwala, A. (ed.), *A History of Legal Informatics* (Saragossa: Prensas Universitarias de Zaragoza, 2010).

Parsons, M., *Effective Knowledge Management for Law Firms* (New York: Oxford University Press, 2004).

Paterson, A., *Lawyers and the Public Good* (Cambridge: Cambridge University Press, 2012).

Pink, D., *A Whole New Mind* (London: Cyan, 2005).

Regan, M. and Heenan, P., 'Supply Chains and Porous Boundaries: The Disaggregation of Legal Services' (2010) *Fordham Law Review* 2137.

Resnik, J. and Curtis, D., *Representing Justice* (New Haven: Yale University Press, 2011).

Sako, M., *General Counsel with Power?* (Oxford: Said Business School, 2011), available at <http://www.sbs.ox.ac.uk/>.

Susskind, R.E., *The Future of Law* (Oxford: Oxford University Press, 1996; paperback edn, 1998).

Susskind, R.E., *Transforming the Law* (Oxford: Oxford University Press, 2000; paperback edn, 2003).

Susskind, R.E., *The End of Lawyers?* (Oxford: Oxford University Press, 2008; paperback edn, 2010).

Tamanaha, B., *Failing Law Schools* (Chicago: University of Chicago Press, 2012).

Wahab, M., Katsh, E., and Rainey, D. (eds), *Online Dispute Resolution: Theory and Practice* (The Hague: Eleven International, 2012).

Woolf, Lord, *Access to Justice—Interim Report and Final Report* (Woolf Inquiry Team, June 2005 and July 2006), available at <http://www.justice.gov.uk/>.

Online resources

<http://lawyermatch.wordpress.com> (Richard Moorfield—research and commentary on the legal professions).

<http://stephenmayson.com> (Stephen Mayson—occasional thoughts about the legal services market).

<http://www.legalfutures.co.uk> (Neil Rose—a guide to conduct, compliance and competence, and the Legal Services Act 2007).

<http://www.law21.ca> (Jordan Furlong—dispatches from a legal profession on the brink).

<http://www.adamsmithesq.com> (Bruce MacEwen—an inquiry into the economics of law firms).

INDEX

180   *Index*

Young lawyers (*Cont.*)
  legal know-how
      providers, 124–125
  legal leasing agencies,
      127–128
  legal management
      consultants, 130–131
  legal process outsourcers
      (LPO), 125–126
  legal publishers, 124
  new-look law firms, 128–129
  online service
      providers, 129–130
  opportunities for the
      future, 131
  overview, 121–122

prospects for the future
    challenges to the profession
        itself, 161–163
    holes or power drills?, 157–159
    shift in legal
        paradigm, 159–161
questions for prospective
    employers
    alternative sourcing, 152
    long-term strategies, 148–149
    overview, 147–148
research and development
    capability, 153–154
role of IT, 152–153
service delivery, 149–150
vision-based thinking, 155–156